pilgrim

LEADER'S GUIDE
A COURSE FOR THE CHRISTIAN JOURNEY

Church Publishing
NEW YORK

The Authors

Stephen Cottrell is the Bishop of Chelmsford
Steven Croft is the Bishop of Sheffield
Paula Gooder is a leading New Testament writer and lecturer
Robert Atwell is the Bishop of Stockport
Sharon Ely Pearson is a Christian educator in The Episcopal Church

pilgrim

LEADER'S GUIDE
A COURSE FOR THE CHRISTIAN JOURNEY

STEPHEN COTTRELL
STEVEN CROFT
PAULA GOODER
ROBERT ATWELL
SHARON ELY PEARSON

Church Publishing
NEW YORK

First published in the United Kingdom in 2013 by

Church House Publishing
Church House
Great Smith Street
London SW1P 3AZ

First published in the United States in 2016 by

Church Publishing, Incorporated.
19 East 34th Street
New York, New York 10016
www.churchpublishing.org

Cover and contents design by David McNeill, Revo Design.

Library of Congress Cataloging-in-Publication Data

A record of this book is available from the Library of Congress.

ISBN-13: 978-0-89869-936-4 (pbk.)
ISBN-13: 978-0-89869-937-1 (ebook)

Printed in the United States of America

CONTENTS

Foreword

The Most Reverend Michael Bruce Curry

Some years ago, while serving as a parish priest in Baltimore, Maryland, I repeatedly noted the slogan on the church vans of one of the local churches. This church made bold witness to the love of God in Jesus through service with and among the poor and in remarkable ways of witness in the life and struggles of the city. The message displayed on the vans as they drove through the heart of the city—in the midst of all of the agony and ecstasy that is urban America—was this: People of the way.

People of the way. Before the church was ever called church, before the community of Jesus was ever called Christian, the Acts of the Apostles in the Bible simply identified the movement of those who followed Jesus as the Way (Acts 9:2).

The truth is that Jesus didn't establish an institution, found a religion, or create an organization. Jesus began a movement! And that movement in its earliest days was called the Way. Being the embodiment of that Way is the reason we are Christian community, church, and even institution. We are to be people of the Jesus way—part of the Jesus movement in the world.

The purpose of the Jesus movement was and is the transformation of the world from the nightmare that often now exists into the dream that God intended since the dawn of creation itself. God really came among us in the person of Jesus of Nazareth. Jesus came to show us the way into that dream of God. Jesus came to show us that the way of God's love is the way to life for us as individuals, communities, nations, and the world.

I am so delighted that *Pilgrim: A Course for the Christian Journey* is now available to The Episcopal Church. Here is a resource that introduces those considering the way of Jesus and more deeply immerses those who have already made that commitment to the Jesus way of life.

Baptized disciples of Jesus are those committed to following the way of Jesus in their lives and witnessing to that way for the sake of God's world. An old hymn of the church says it best:

Come, labor on.
Claim the high calling angels cannot share—
to young and old the Gospel gladness bear;
redeem the time; its hours too swiftly fly.
The night draws nigh.
Come, labor on.

No time for rest, till glows the western sky,
till the long shadows o'er our pathway lie,
and a glad sound comes with the setting sun,—
"Servants, well done." (The Hymnal 1982, #541)

God bless you, and keep the faith,

+Michael B. Curry

pilgrim

PART ONE:
WELCOME TO *PILGRIM*

An Overview

Pilgrim is a course for the Christian journey. The aim of the course is to help people become disciples of Jesus Christ.

A pilgrim is a person on a journey. The Bible is a book full of journeys. God's people are always traveling. God's call to Abraham was to leave his own land for a great journey of faith. God's call to Moses was to lead God's people on a journey from slavery in Egypt to freedom in the promised land. Jesus took his first disciples on a journey from Galilee to Jerusalem. One of the earliest names for the people called Christians was followers of the Way.

Pilgrim is designed to help every local church to invite others to join the people of God on our great journey of faith. Its purpose is to help you to draw together a small group of people who are inquiring about Christian faith or are new to faith and to help them learn about the faith together.

This leader's guide is for clergy and church leaders who are thinking about introducing *Pilgrim* into the life of their church and is also a short handbook for those who will lead the groups.

Why *Pilgrim?*

Lifelong Christian faith formation in The Episcopal Church is lifelong growth in the knowledge, service, and love of God as followers of Christ and is informed by Scripture, tradition, and reason. As stated in the Charter for Lifelong Christian Formation, God invites all people:

● To enter into a prayerful life of worship, continuous learning, intentional outreach, advocacy, and service

● To hear the Word of God through Scripture, to honor church teachings, and continually to embrace the joy of Baptism and

Eucharist, spreading the Good News of the risen Christ and minister to all

- To respond to the needs of our constantly changing communities, as Jesus calls us, in ways that reflect our diversity and cultures as we seek, wonder, and discover together

- To hear what the Spirit is saying to God's people, placing ourselves in the stories of our faith, thereby empowering us to proclaim the Gospel message.

Pilgrim has been developed to help make new disciples and strengthen the understanding of discipleship to all who choose to deepen their understanding of the Christian journey and where they are on their own faith journey.

The structure of *Pilgrim*

There are many different aspects to helping people learn about the Christian faith.

We have taken as our starting point Jesus' summary of the commandments. We are called to offer our lives to God through loving God with all our mind, soul, strength, and heart and to love our neighbor as ourselves. Learning about Christian faith and growing in Christian faith is about more than what we believe. It's also about the ways in which we pray and develop our relationship with God, about the way we live our lives, and about living in God's vision for the Church and for the world.

We offer two stages of material in *Pilgrim*. There are four short *Pilgrim* books (each comprising a course of six or seven sessions) in the Follow Stage, designed for those who are inquirers and very new to the faith. Then there are four short *Pilgrim* books (each comprising a six-session course) in the Grow Stage, designed for those who want to go further and learn more.

The structure of *Pilgrim* is set out in the diagram.

PILGRIM			
A Course for the Christian Journey			
	What do Christians believe?	How do Christians know and worship God?	How do Christians live?	What is the Christian vision for the world?
FOLLOW STAGE *"Do you turn to Jesus Christ?"*	❶ TURNING TO CHRIST	❷ THE LORD'S PRAYER	❸ THE COMMANDMENTS	❹ THE BEATITUDES
GROW STAGE *"Will you continue in the Apostles teaching and fellowship?"*	❺ THE CREEDS	❻ THE EUCHARIST	❼ THE BIBLE	❽ CHURCH AND KINGDOM
	Doctrine	Spirituality	Ethics	Lifestyle

Each short course consists of six or seven sessions. The courses in the Follow Stage are designed to be led by someone who is further on in their Christian faith and who is a skilled teacher. The courses in the Grow Stage are designed so that the group can lead and guide themselves with some external help and support.

In the Follow Stage, each of the four courses is structured around one of four key texts:

- the Baptismal Covenant
- the Lord's Prayer
- the Commandments
- the Beatitudes

These four texts have been important in helping people in the early stages of their Christian journey since the earliest days of the Christian faith.

In the Grow Stage, each of the four courses is structured around a major theme of the Christian life:

- the Creeds
- the Sacraments
- the Scriptures
- living in God's Church and in God's world

Each session of each course is rooted in shared prayer. Each session begins with the group exploring the Scriptures together and continues with a more sustained reflection on the theme and opportunity for questions and discussion.

The short courses in the four Follow Stage books can be approached in any order. Together, we believe they offer a balanced introduction to the Christian life and journey. Our hope and prayer is that *Pilgrim* will help to introduce people to the Christian Way and also equip them to live their whole lives as disciples of Jesus Christ.

About this Leader's Guide

This guide is both an introduction to *Pilgrim* and a guide to using it well. The next section, Part Two: Teaching the Faith, explores some of the ideas behind the course and the principles that have guided its development. Part Three: Leading a *Pilgrim* Group is a more practical guide to gathering and leading a group on one or more short courses. Part Four: *Pilgrim* Resources offers liturgical resources, additional books to support the various topics in *Pilgrim*, and An Outline of the Faith, commonly called the Catechism from the Book of Common Prayer. Finally, Part Five offers some powerful images and an understanding of the role of the teacher, the group leader, and catechist in this process of making new disciples.

pilgrim

PART TWO:
TEACHING THE FAITH

Catechesis

Catechesis is a word used throughout Christian history for special teaching offered to Christians who are preparing for baptism or who are newly baptized. It's an unfamiliar word to most people today but well worth learning. It is pronounced *kat-e-KEY-sis*.

It is Luke who first uses the term *catechesis* to describe the special teaching given to new Christians. Luke dedicates his gospel to Theophilus:

> so that you may know the truth concerning the things about which you have been instructed [literally, *catechized*].
>
> LUKE 1:4

In Acts, Luke introduces Apollos as someone who had been "instructed (literally, catechized) in the way of the Lord" (Acts 18:25), though he remained in need of further teaching.

Much of the New Testament, including the Gospels, was written to support this great work of catechesis, the early instruction of new disciples both before and immediately after their baptism. Many of the early creeds and formulas we know from the New Testament were also developed to support this work of teaching the faith to those who were learning it for the first time.

In the early centuries of the Christian faith, the gospel spread and the Church grew in a context that was often hostile and difficult. It was a costly thing to be a Christian. Careful preparation and support was essential both before and after baptism. The Early Church therefore developed ways of teaching the faith and making disciples centered on preparation for baptism and gave this work the name of the catechumenate. Many of the great traditions of the Christian Church began as a way of supporting those who were learning the faith for the first time. In particular, the season of Lent was originally a time of preparation for baptism at Easter, kept by the whole Church in support of the candidates.

The Catechism

All down the centuries, in periods of mission and growth, the Church in every tradition has always paid particular attention to the task of catechesis and to *what* should be taught to new Christians in the form of the different *catechisms*.

A catechism is a way of the Church ensuring together that new Christians learn all that they need to learn in preparation for their baptism and for a lifetime of Christian discipleship.

The Episcopal Church has its own catechism, called An Outline of the Faith. This form of teaching had been included in previous prayer books, but what is now provided in the Book of Common Prayer (1979) is a substantially expanded and revised version of these catechisms. It is reproduced at the end of this book (pp. 81–100).

The notes concerning the catechism in the 1979 prayer book state that this catechism has two intended uses. First, it is a teaching aid for clergy and lay catechists (teachers), "to give an outline for instruction," perhaps for confirmation classes or newcomers to the Episcopal Church. It cautions that the catechism is not a "complete statement of belief and practice" but rather "a point of departure for the teacher," who can use its question-and-answer format as a way of beginning a discussion on various aspects of the Christian faith and life. It poses fundamental questions that can begin a deeper conversation, such as:

- What does it mean to be created in the image of God?
- What is sin?
- What is prayer?

Many of us may remember catechism or confirmation classes from our youth in which we were expected to memorize the answers in the catechism in order to pass our "test" at confirmation. Times have changed, however, and the 1979 prayer book suggests the catechism is provided "for ease of reference" (BCP, 844), not for memorization and recitation.

The second use suggested by the prayer book concerns those who are new to the Episcopal Church, "to provide a brief summary of the Church's teaching for an inquiring stranger who picks up a Prayer Book" (BCP, 844). Since the first encounter many people have with the Episcopal Church is an occasion when they attend one of our liturgical services—baptism, marriage, burial, perhaps a Sunday Eucharist—it makes sense to include a general outline of what we believe within the covers of the first book newcomers will hold during their visit.

Other Church traditions have their own catechisms. The best known (and the longest) is the *Catechism of the Catholic Church*, first published in 1992, which runs to 700 pages in the standard English edition (Burns & Oates, 2000).

The *Catechism of the Catholic Church* has four sections:

1 The Creeds (the content or object of our faith based on the Nicene and Apostles' Creeds)

2 The Sacred Liturgy (how we celebrate and communicate the faith based around worship and an exposition of seven sacraments)

3 The Christian way of life (how we live out our faith based around the Commandments)

4 Christian Prayer (how we deepen our relationship with God based around the Lord's Prayer)

Unlike An Outline of the Faith, commonly called The Catechism in The Episcopal Church, the *Catechism of the Catholic Church* is primarily intended as a guide for the whole Church in the great task of catechesis, not as a manual to be placed in the hands of those learning the faith for the first time.

Why do we need new material?

In every generation, the Church needs to reflect on this great task of catechesis and the way in which we make disciples. This is especially true in seasons of significant renewal in the life of the Church or times of change in our wider society or periods of great missionary endeavor.

Many people would argue that the present time is one when the life of The Episcopal Church needs to be renewed (and is being renewed) for the task we face. All would agree that we are living through times of great change in our society and the place of Christian faith within it. This is also a time when the Church is called to engage in God's mission, including the mission to make disciples, with fresh energy, creativity, and zeal in the power of the Holy Spirit.

However, the Church is called to reflect on our methods and resources for catechesis, especially for the sake of the people in our own generation as we invite them to follow Jesus Christ and become his disciples.

The *Pilgrim* Way

We have tried to develop material that is suitable for catechesis in the twenty-first century. We believe there are eleven distinctive characteristics.

Pilgrim starts at the very beginning.

Many adults, children, and young people who are open to exploring faith know very little about the faith when they begin that journey of exploration. For that reason, we need material that begins at the beginning, which assumes very little knowledge or understanding but simply a desire to learn and explore from first principles.

That means that for most people there is quite a lot to learn. We have prepared eight short courses. Four are for those starting out on the journey as inquirers and are called the Follow Stage of *Pilgrim*. The second four build on the first, and we have called this the Grow Stage.

A group could tackle the material in any order but it makes most sense to work through the Follow courses before the Grow material and for all groups to begin with the first course, *Turning to Christ*.

Pilgrim is about our whole lives.

Living as a Christian is about more than simply believing a set of doctrines. Living as a disciple is about the whole of our lives. Much of the material currently used for teaching inquirers and new believers is fundamentally shaped by the Creeds. This element in catechesis is important. However, we believe our material needs to be balanced to help new disciples to pray and develop their relationship with God; to share fully in the life of the Church; and to live out their discipleship and ministry in the world. Catechesis needs to pay due attention to each of these aspects of the Christian life.

Each of these dimensions also needs to be reflected if possible in the life of the group. This means that, when the group meets, it will not simply be for study but will be about building community, praying together as faith grows, serving together, and supporting one another in living out our discipleship.

Pilgrim focuses on following Jesus Christ.

At the heart of catechesis we find, in essence, a Person, the Person of Jesus of Nazareth, the only Son from the Father, who suffered and died for us and who now, after rising, is living with us forever. To catechize is to reveal in the Person of Christ the whole of God's eternal design reaching fulfilment in that Person.

CATECHISM OF THE CATHOLIC CHURCH

Catechesis needs to be comprehensive but also clearly focused on equipping people to follow Jesus Christ as disciples in the whole of their lives. Catechesis is not a course in theology as an academic exercise. Catechesis is about being formed and shaped in the pattern of Christ and, in Paul's words, about Christ being formed and shaped in us (Galatians 4:19).

A correct understanding is essential but cannot be divorced from a life that is being transformed and made whole and lived according to God's call. Taking part in a *Pilgrim* group should lead to change both for the members of the group and for the leaders.

Pilgrim flows from the Scriptures.

Christians believe that God is revealed to us in the Scriptures and supremely in the person of Jesus Christ, God's living Word, who is himself at the very heart of the Scriptures, God's written Word.

> All scripture is inspired by God [literally "God-breathed"] and is useful for teaching, for reproof, for correction and for training in righteousness so that everyone who belongs to God may be proficient and equipped for every good work.
>
> 2 TIMOTHY 3:16

Catechesis therefore needs to take the Scriptures seriously and introduce inquirers and new believers to a lifetime of engagement with the Scriptures through reading the Bible together. The primary focus of each session of *Pilgrim* is a group of people engaging together in reading the Bible and attending to Scripture together through careful reading of the text.

Some material for catechesis focuses simply on one part of Scripture, most commonly one of the gospels. However, it is important that a new Christian is helped to read, understand, and interpret the whole of the Scriptures as part of the Church.

Through the different sections of the course we have introduced a range of different Scriptures, from both Old and New Testaments (from the law, the prophets, the writings, the gospels, and the epistles) so that the participants begin to gain a rich, textured understanding of the Bible and learn to love reading the Scriptures as part of their discipleship.

Pilgrim draws deeply from the Christian tradition.

In The Episcopal Church in the twenty-first century we stand in a long tradition of catechesis, which stretches back to the apostles. That tradition has much to teach us.

Pilgrim seeks to be faithful to that tradition in two ways. The first is by focusing on four key texts in the Follow Stage, and building on these in the Grow Stage. In the catechumenates of the Early Church these four texts were passed on and handed over (the root meaning of tradition) as a key part of preparation for baptism:

● **The Creeds**—the Baptismal Covenant is used in the Follow Stage and the Apostles' and Nicene Creeds in the Grow Stage.

● **The Lord's Prayer**—leading into the Eucharist in the Grow Stage.

● **The Commandments**—leading into the Scriptures in the Grow Stage.

● **The Beatitudes**—leading into a vision of the kingdom of God in the Grow Stage.

In addition, a whole range of authors from Christian history are included, with extracts, readings, and prayers in each session giving a sense of the breadth and depth of Christian vision and providing a gateway to future learning and reflection.

Pilgrim honors the Episcopal way.

Jesus Christ calls us not to solitary discipleship but to be disciples in community. Every disciple belongs to the one, holy, catholic, and apostolic Church. However, we are also called to belong to a specific Church.

Over many centuries, the Holy Spirit has called and shaped the life of the Christian Churches in different ways. At the beginning of Christian discipleship it is more important to understand one way in depth, and to become part of that way, than to understand many different ways superficially.

Pilgrim was originally written to be a specifically Anglican resource which follows Anglican belief and practice at every point. The Episcopal Church is part of the Anglican Communion, and thus the program has been adapted for an Episcopal audience. In the footsteps of _Pilgrim's_ originators, we hope and pray that it will be useful to Episcopalians in the United States as well as those provinces and dioceses that are part of The Episcopal Church around the world. We trust that the material may be helpful to other Christians of other traditions. However, we have not attempted to disguise who we are. _Pilgrim_ is written in the hope that it will be used by God and by God's people to form disciples in an Episcopal tradition of being Christian.

What this means will be seen more fully from the materials themselves. However, we would highlight the Episcopal / Anglican values that have shaped this material:

1 The importance of reading and engaging with the whole of Scripture in both Old and New Testaments

2 The valuing and balancing of Scripture, tradition, reason, and experience in all reflection on faith and understanding

3 The teaching of the whole and historic Christian faith as summarized in the Apostles' and Nicene Creeds

4   Valuing especially the sacraments given by Jesus (Eucharist and Baptism)

5   The joys of liturgical worship inviting the participation of the whole people of God in the praise of God's glory

6   A call to engage in God's mission to the whole of creation (as described in the Anglican Communion's five marks of mission)

7   A recognition that the whole people of God are called to discipleship and ministry each according to their gifts and vocation and to sharing in the governance and leadership of God's people

8   A recognition of the threefold order of deacon, priest, and bishop in the ordering of the life of God's Church

9   A recognition that the outcome of discipleship and mission is community, social, and cultural change around the world

10 A recognition of the importance of local culture in a global context for interpreting Scripture, discipleship, and mission

Pilgrim helps people to learn in different ways.

There are many different ways to help people learn about the Christian faith. We have set out in Learning the Faith some of the principles that have guided our own approach to teaching and learning (pp. 33–38).

With the changing role of the Christian faith in our society, it seems particularly important to offer material and a method for catechesis which creates at the same time a level playing field between different members of a group and a community where people learn and grow together as partners in discipleship and as equals in faith.

In previous generations, Christian faith was commonly taught from a position of authority from an authorized and learned preacher or teacher imparting knowledge to (largely silent) students or learners. In our present context, such an approach is unlikely to be fruitful.

Adult learning is now much more about active engagement and pooled experience, and this is especially so in the area of faith.

Those who come to learn will almost certainly learn best in many different ways. A variety of approaches is vital in any single group. Anyone leading a group must be free to tailor the approach to their own particular group of learners. One of the tests of Christian faith is that the faith is seen to be authentic and lived out in the experience of those who teach. The group leaders therefore need to be willing to share themselves and their own experience and questions of faith in order to guide and lead the group well. The material provided for the group to work with must be flexible and adaptable to local need.

For this reason, the Scriptures are set out at the heart of *Pilgrim* as the primary teacher and source of reflection and instruction. Reading Scripture together and listening together to what the Spirit is saying to the Church creates a level playing field. It offers an experience where the whole group bring their insights, experience, questions, and wisdom and learn together in community, initially with guidance from more experienced Christians.

Reading and reflection on Scripture together is followed in each session by a written reflection from one of a range of different voices in the Anglican tradition. Bishops, theologians, and educators contribute these essays to draw on a range of different sources and the whole rich variety of the Church. The aim of these reflections is to help the group to learn individually and together about one or other aspect of the faith.

We hope the "feel" of the group will be similar to other adult group learning experiences in contemporary society such as book groups, support groups, or AA meetings.

Pilgrim helps disciples to go on learning for all of their lives.

The best catechesis creates a lifelong appetite for learning about the Christian faith in many different ways. So we hope that each of the eight short courses in the material will create a thirst for the next and that the whole set of material will form and shape disciples who know that they have much more to learn, and commit to that continuous process of learning, growing, and changing throughout their lives.

Specifically, we envision that the first four courses in the Follow Stage will be led by skilled group leaders trained and equipped to lead others in catechesis. However, we also hope that through these first four sections of the course, each group will become a learning community, and that new leaders will emerge who can guide the group through the Grow Stage of the course and on into further learning and life together into the future. _Follow_ is therefore a tool not simply for the catechesis of individuals but for the formation of small mission-shaped Christian communities, which are the building blocks of the life of the local church.

Pilgrim can be used by every tradition in The Episcopal Church.

Reading and reflection on Scripture together is followed in each session by a written reflection from one of a range of different voices in the Anglican tradition. Bishops, theologians, and educators contribute these essays to draw on a range of different sources and the whole rich variety of the Church.

Our aim has been to provide material that can be used fruitfully in a very wide variety of settings. We don't think it will always be the best material for every situation. However, as authors we believe there will be real advantages in having good quality material which can be used across the different traditions and contexts of Church, in fresh expressions of Church and parishes, cathedrals and chaplaincies, and which is able to draw men and women and young people into a common experience of what it means to be a disciple of Jesus Christ in the Episcopal tradition.

Pilgrim can be used with young people and adults.

Our hope and prayer is that *Pilgrim* can be used effectively with groups of young people as well as with adult groups (or with groups that mix the two). However, some additional adaptation might be needed when working with younger teenagers.

Pilgrim is realistic in its use of resources.

Some churches are outwardly rich in resources for catechesis, and others are, on the surface, less well off. Resources include finances for materials, locations to meet in, and most of all people available to help lead and support the life of the nurture groups.

Pilgrim has been designed to serve a variety of contexts and especially those where there are outwardly few resources. All you need is a copy of the course book for each person; a copy of this leader's guide for the group leaders, a room to meet in, and some light refreshments. You can, of course add things as you have them (such as a meal together, a retreat, or a day away), but these are not essential.

If even these resources seem beyond your church we would encourage you to look at two things carefully.

The first is to explore again your understanding of God's grace and the rich gifts of ministry God gives to the Church. There are many instances in the Bible of God's people having very few resources, but God providing all that is needed and more as people move forward in faith. The story of the feeding of the multitude in John 6 is a good place to begin. What are five barley loaves and two fish among so many? Give thanks for what you have, pray, and believe and be surprised at what God will provide.

The second is to review your priorities individually and as a church. Where are the time, energy, and resources going if you do not have the time and resources as a church of The Episcopal Church to offer one opportunity each year for new people to learn more about the Christian faith? In many congregations, this situation has become so normal which is in reality a scandal.

Read and teach the Gospels again and especially be alert to the priority Jesus gives to those who are lost. Luke 15 is a good place to begin. Ask yourself what priorities Jesus would set for the Church. Then take action together.

An Annual Rhythm

It is vital to recognize the importance of catechesis in this task of growing the Church.

In all of our talk about mission action-planning and strategies for growth, there is one key critical event. That critical event takes place when lay or ordained ministers gather a small group of people who are inquiring about the Christian faith and want to learn more. The group may be just two or three people or a dozen. Together the group journeys and explores the Christian gospel in such a way that people are able to make a response of faith and become Christians and they move on to be established and equipped as disciples.

Where this critical event is happening over and over again in a regular cycle, there will be people in your church coming to faith and growing in faith. Where that is happening the church is likely to be growing in numbers and depth of service. But where this critical event of catechesis is not happening, no amount of strategy and planning for ministry can replace it. A refocusing of the energy of lay and ordained ministers on ministry catechesis is absolutely vital for the growth of the Church in the twenty-first century.

It doesn't matter whether the church in question is urban or rural, a cathedral or a newly planted church. For the church to be growing there must be an intentional focusing of time and energy in the ministry of catechesis.

The importance of this work is born out in a number of studies where only one significant common factor has emerged so far in relation to spiritual and numerical growth in congregations: the frequency of offering nurture groups (which is at the heart of catechesis). It is no coincidence that the same factor is highly significant in the overall morale and role satisfaction of the clergy.

But how can catechesis become more central in the ordinary life of every Episcopal expression of Church in the present day? There are many competing demands on time and energy. One answer is to return to first principles and to begin to make good use again of the cycle of the Christian year.

The diagram on page 30 shows a way of doing this that we recommend. The year is divided into three seasons, using the agricultural picture that is common in the Gospels and in Paul's writings (see Matthew 13 and 1 Corinthians 3:5-9).

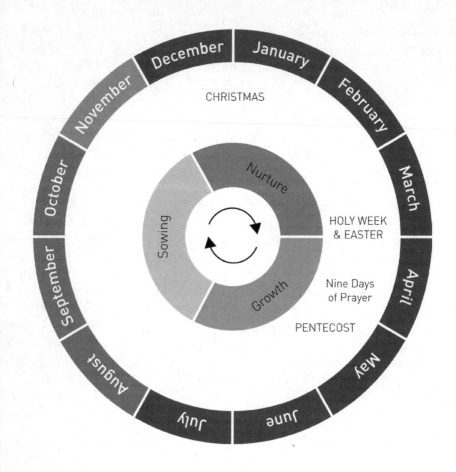

Sowing

The season of sowing the seed of the gospel occurs throughout the church year, but it is in the spring, summer, and early autumn that we are immersed in new growth through God's creation all around us. There are many ways we can continue this growth in the life of the church through celebrations and activities for all ages; through Rogation Days, Vacation Bible Schools, and mission trips; through ministry with families bringing children to be baptized, coming to be married, and through ministry with the bereaved throughout the year; through special outreach events or a regular program of visiting others. Come autumn, we rededicate ourselves to a new program year as well as a focus on giving thanks to God for the harvest and abundance that we have received.

Nurture

The season set aside for nurturing the faith of inquirers and new Christians can occur at any time, however mid-autumn through Lent and leading up to Easter is the time of year to draw together the different contacts made through sowing the seed of the gospel throughout the year into one [or several] nurture groups. Lent was originally a time of intense preparation for baptism for new adult candidates. In the Episcopal Church it is also a time for the preparation of candidates for confirmation and a renewal of baptismal vows. The first four courses of *Pilgrim* are designed for exactly this kind of group.

Each short course is six weeks long (or, in the case of *Turning to Christ*, seven weeks) so the material can be used by offering the first course to the group in the six weeks before Christmas, a second in the six weeks between Christmas and Lent, a third course in Lent itself and finally the fourth course between Easter and Pentecost.

Growth

Third, every church community needs to offer ways in which every disciple can continue to grow and develop and be stretched in their faith.

This may happen through the creation of ongoing small communities of faith which continue to meet and guide themselves through the Discipleship material and thereafter use other material for their learning and growth. Or it may happen through the offering of times of learning for the whole church family outside of Sunday worship between Easter or Pentecost, and the summer. These might include study days, retreats, parish pilgrimages, or weekends away.

Prayer

Finally, this whole pattern of catechesis needs to be rooted and grounded in the prayer of the whole people of God. One helpful way to focus this is to use the nine days between Ascension and Pentecost each year as a nine-day (or novena) period of prayer especially for the making of disciples and the growth of the Church.

The Episcopal Church is in the midst of a profound transition to once again become a Church in mission, making disciples as a normal and natural part of our common life. A key part of this transition is relearning this deep rhythm of catechesis, and setting that rhythm at the heart of our common life together so that every local Christian community sees itself again as a school for the Lord's service, a place where disciples are made, and a community where people regularly find faith in Jesus Christ. A key task of lay and ordained ministers (but especially the ordained) is to lead this work of catechesis and ensure that this rhythm of teaching the faith grows and deepens with the years.

In many places, these core disciplines of sowing the seed of the gospel, nurturing the faith of inquirers and new believers, and teaching the whole people of God are alive and well. These are the places where the The Episcopal Church is healthy and growing. In many other places, these disciplines have been sorely neglected and urgently need to be revived and practiced by the whole people of God until they become again a normal and natural part of church life. Beginning to work with *Pilgrim* is a way of re-engaging with these core disciplines, which need to be present in every community.

The sequence is never neat or exact, of course. In the last analysis it doesn't really matter whether you offer your nurture group in October or May. It is unlikely that in any given year an individual would engage with the local church as the seed is sown, then join a nurture group, then share in growth. The vital thing is that all three core disciplines are practiced in an ongoing way, owned by the Church and undergirded with prayer.

Learning the Faith

Different patterns of catechesis are based around different educational methodology. It is important for the group leaders to know that the authors have tried to work with an explicit but evolving methodology which we believe is helpful and appropriate for the times in which we live and faithful to the broader Christian and specifically Anglican tradition in which we are working.

We have a working list of seven basic principles.

1 **God is revealed gradually to those who follow God, and God's call comes in different ways to different people.**

   The divine plan of Revelation is realized simultaneously by deeds and words which are intrinsically bound up with each other and shed light on each other. It involves a specific, divine pedagogy. God communicates himself to man gradually. He prepares him to welcome by stages the supernatural Revelation that is to culminate in the person and mission of the incarnate Word, Jesus Christ.

   CATECHISM OF THE CATHOLIC CHURCH

God's great plan of revelation unfolds gradually in the Scriptures and culminates in God's revelation through Jesus Christ. In the same way, in many individual encounters within the Scriptures we see God being revealed step by step to those who would follow Jesus.

The journey of the disciples in the gospels is one of gradual discovery and of seeing who Jesus is. On the Road to Emmaus we witness Jesus revealing himself to the two disciples who walk with him gradually through listening and loving attention, through Scripture, and finally in the breaking of the bread (Luke 24). In the Acts of the Apostles, we share in Peter's ongoing discovery of the cosmic significance of Christ as he is led to understand what God is doing even among the Gentiles (Acts 10).

We also see in the Scriptures the ways in which God deals with different people. Some are called who are willing to serve and surrender themselves, like the prophet Isaiah who declares: "Here I am; send me!" (Isaiah 6:8). Others are called who are resistant to different ministries and aware of their own inadequacies.

There are moments of clarity and encounter with God in most journeys to Christian faith. These are always part of a longer process or journey. Sometimes they are in continuity with what has gone before. At other times there is a discontinuity and a sudden turning around (as in Saul's conversion on the Road to Damascus, Acts 9).

Those who work with people first coming to faith need to be alert to these different ways in which God works in human lives and to be open to the many different ways in which people experience the grace of God. Catechesis forms a living community where people are enabled to share this experience with others and so understand it more fully.

2 **To become a Christian is to encounter the risen Christ in the Scriptures, in Christian community, in personal prayers, and in the Eucharist. That encounter is life-changing.**

The roads people follow to faith are different but the end point is the same. The goal of all Christian catechesis is to enable men and women to encounter the risen Christ, to place their faith in him, to receive salvation, and to follow Jesus Christ as his disciples.

This encounter with the risen Christ happens in many different ways, but four means of grace in particular are identified in the Scriptures and remain vital in the life of the Church.

Those who became Christians on the day of Pentecost "devoted themselves to the apostles teaching and fellowship, to the breaking of bread and the prayers" (Acts 2:42).

Catechesis must take seriously this need to encounter the risen Christ through these four means of grace especially, and so be founded on Scripture, intentionally nurture Christian community, draw people into participation in the Eucharist, and be set in the context of living prayer.

Those who lead groups for catechesis need to be prepared to share something of themselves and also be prepared to grow small Christian communities as a key focus of their work.

3 **Growing in Christian faith is therefore not simply about growth in understanding but is growth in character, in relationship, in response to God's grace, and in community.**

According to Jesus, the kingdom of God is like a mustard seed "which, when it is sown upon the ground, is the smallest of all the seeds of the earth. Yet when it is sown it grows up and becomes the greatest of all shrubs, and puts forth large branches, so that the birds of the air can make nests in its shade" (Mark 4:31-32).

Transformation happens in a variety of ways as a person comes to know Christ. However, it will not only be a transformation of understanding. There may be specific sins from the past to be confessed and forgiven as part of coming to faith. Aspects of a person's lifestyle may need to be set right. Relationships may need to be healed and set right and forgiveness extended for past hurts. Order may need to be brought to chaotic lives.

These things will not happen in a moment. Growth in grace is the work of a lifetime. However, those who are involved in catechesis will need to help those preparing for baptism and confirmation to discern God's grace in their lives and to grow in these ways as they explore the Way.

4 The way in which we begin to learn about the Christian faith will condition and affect the way in which we continue to learn and grow in faith.

In any learning experience, we learn more through the informal or hidden curriculum than through the formal learning.

A group formed for catechesis will therefore communicate important lessons to those who come about the Christian life which are nothing to do with what is on the printed page of the material. These lessons will be contained in the culture and the atmosphere set by the group leaders.

Is every person's contribution welcomed? Is prayer taken seriously? Is there a genuine interest in everyone? Is the content presented at an understandable level? Is there a practical application to what is being learned?

Those leading this work of catechesis need to be aware of this responsibility and provide the best environment they can for laying the foundations of discipleship.

5 The Holy Spirit is at work in the task of catechesis, through the common life of the group, through the Scriptures, the living word of God, and in the lives of individual group members.

One of the striking lessons of the New Testament is that neither Jesus himself nor Paul spend more than a few years with any group of disciples. Although learning and discipleship is a lifetime's task, initial formation and catechesis never seem to take longer than two or three years.

The reason for this is twofold. The first and most important is that God gives the Holy Spirit to every member of the Body of Christ. The Spirit's role is to dwell within the believer, to equip them for ministry and to "teach you everything and remind you of all that I have said to you" (John 14:26).

The second reason is that the purpose of catechesis is not to create disciples who are dependent on those who teach them but disciples who are mature enough to take their place in the Body of Christ and in the world, and exercise gifts and ministries, including leading others to faith.

It is vital therefore that all those involved in catechesis are focused on the end goal of creating mature, interdependent groups of disciples rather than Christians who are forever pastorally dependent on others. It is also vital that all new Christians are introduced to and experience the life and work of the Holy Spirit following the pattern of the apostles (Acts 2:38, 8:14-16, 18:26-27 and 19:1-7).

6   To be a disciple is to be a lifelong learner of truths about the faith. Catechesis should therefore prepare the group for this lifetime of discipleship.

Again the Scriptures bear witness to the call to every Christian to continue to learn and to grow in wisdom through the whole of life.

Catechesis must avoid the sense that a period of instruction about the Christian life leads then to a later period when there is no need to go on learning and growing. There is always more to know of God and to learn about the Christian way. The circumstances and cycle of our lives mean that the gospel will mean different things in early life, in middle years, and in old age. There is a need to continue growing continuously in our discipleship.

Catechesis must therefore point beyond itself to the lifelong commitment to learning and to grow as a disciple.

7 **God's call is to know God as Father, Son, and Holy Spirit and to enjoy God for ever. However, God's call is also to a lifetime of offering ourselves in Christian discipleship. Catechesis is about helping a new Christian recognize and receive God's grace and gifts and to begin to exercise their gifts in ministry and explore their vocation.**

Growth in understanding as a Christian must embrace the call to whole life discipleship; the call to offer our best gifts to God and our time and resources in God's service.

As Paul writes in Romans:

> I appeal to you therefore, brothers and sisters, by the mercies of God, to present your bodies as a living sacrifice, holy and acceptable to God, which is your spiritual worship. [2]Do not be conformed to this world but be transformed by the renewing of your minds, so that you may discern what is the will of God—what is good and acceptable and perfect.
>
> ROMANS 12:1-2

pilgrim

PART THREE:
LEADING A *PILGRIM* GROUP

Gathering a Group Together

How then should you begin to draw a small group of people together to be part of a *Pilgrim* group?

You will need to plan four or five months in advance. Don't wait until you have five expressions of interest from inquirers and then arrange the group. Plan in faith that as you are praying and sowing the seed of the gospel, so there will be some kind of harvest of people who want to find out more. And aim for this to happen on an annual basis.

Putting on a *Pilgrim* group can become a normal part of the annual cycle of congregational life as you weave the work of evangelism, catechesis, and discipleship into the fabric of church ministry. So put the dates in the church calendar in advance and sort out the practical questions of when and where you will meet. Make sure the venue and time are suitable for those whom you envision might come.

Also decide in advance who the leaders of the group will be. Ideally you need at least two people and, if possible, three. Their commitment is to work with the group through the first stage of the material. They will between them help gather the group together, lead the sessions, and, most importantly of all, help the group to become a community. To do this they will need to be committed to the group for up to a year. Perhaps one or more leaders might want to journey beyond that as the group enters the second stage of *Pilgrim*, focusing on discipleship.

Those leading the group will offer different gifts, but at least one should have the skills to facilitate a small group learning together and to guide the agenda of each evening. This normally means some theological training, so it is helpful if your team of leaders includes someone who is ordained or a trained Christian educator, licensed catechist, a graduate of the Education for Ministry (EfM) program, or someone who has experience and training for this sort of ministry. But not all the leaders need these gifts.

The leaders should have time to get to know the group members and to help them grow in their own faith and discipleship. Sharing in leading a group of this kind is a great privilege and it's not usually hard to find people for the role. There may be someone in the church who has the potential for this ministry and who needs to learn on the job as an apprentice.

The nature and purpose of the group needs to be communicated to the whole church. If the whole community understands what this group is for then they are more likely to have the confidence to suggest it to family and friends or to come themselves. Here is a sample description you could use on your church website or in your weekly bulletin.

Pilgrim

Once a year St. John's offers a group for inquirers and new Christians who want to learn more about the Christian faith.

This year the group will meet on Thursday evenings in the church lounge at 7:30 pm starting on November 1st. The initial commitment is for six weeks, but we hope to go on meeting through to May of next year. The group is for:

● those who have recently started coming to church

● those who want the chance to think about Christian faith

● those preparing for baptism or confirmation

● those who have been Christians for many years and want to visit the roots of their faith again

This year the *Pilgrim* group will be led by Dave Jones, Miranda Smith, and Mike Smith. For more information contact the number or email below or speak to us after church.

Please pass on this news to anyone you know who may be interested.

You will want to spread the net wide and make the group as well known as you can through posters, the church bulletin, and some simple printed invitations.

Most people will come only if the publicity material is backed up with a conversation and a personal invitation from the person who knows them best already in the life of the church, perhaps supported by a conversation with the group leaders.

How the conversation goes will of course depend on the two people involved. It may be helpful to emphasize:

- that no commitment to Christian faith or knowledge of faith is involved at the beginning
- there are lots of opportunities to ask questions
- everyone will be in the same boat
- it's a good chance to get to know people
- everyone at some point in their lives would benefit from exploring the Christian faith in this kind of way
- no one will be put on the spot
- most people find this kind of group really enjoyable

You may want to include a meal as part of the evening, depending on the setting and the resources you have available. But whatever you do, hospitality will be a key ingredient, and someone needs to be responsible for organizing refreshments of some sort at each session.

Sometimes it can be helpful if an inquirer comes with someone who is already a Christian and member of the church. Some churches formalize this and call these people *sponsors*. But it is best not to have a hard and fast rule about it. This is a detail to be worked out locally.

There may be some practical questions to address, such as offers of help with childcare or transportation.

People learn in different ways. For that reason it's always helpful to have a resource box of short books and DVDs of talks; Christian music on CD; and details of other events taking place which the group may find useful as the course moves forward. You will find resources listed in the back of this book as well as in each of the course participant books.

The most important preparation is prayer. Paul writes in 1 Corinthians 3:6: "I planted, Apollos watered, but God gave the growth." This informal gathering of a handful of people is providing an opportunity and place where men and women can encounter the truth of the gospel and the power of the living God.

Make sure that others in the life of the church are praying for the group and for its leaders both as you gather people together and as the group begins to meet. Experience suggests that in this kind of ministry it is wise to expect setbacks of different kinds. There may often be a sense of spiritual conflict and struggle as you seek to provide this safe and secure environment to learn about the Christian faith and to build community. When that happens, keep praying, and keep going. It's often a sign that you are on exactly the right track.

Leading the Sessions

The *Pilgrim* material is designed to be flexible and adaptable. This includes the time you take for each session. The material will fit into an hour, but in preparing the material we've had a 75- to 90-minute session in mind, so you may need to do some pruning if you decide an hour is better for your context. Don't feel you have to do everything.

Each leader needs a copy of this leader's guide; and each group member a copy of the member's booklet for the course. People don't need to read it beforehand, though bear in mind quite a few will. Once they have the book, it is inevitable that they will look ahead. In some groups there may be people who are uncomfortable with written material. Bear this in mind. In some cases you may decide to dispense with the booklet altogether and just use it as your guide. But these cases will be rare.

The first time you use the material you'll need at least one planning meeting for the leaders to plan the sessions themselves (as well as the initial planning meeting that was about drawing the group together). You may want to briefly review each session between meetings and reflect on what has worked well and what hasn't.

Each session of the course follows a similar pattern.

Refreshments as people arrive can be very helpful in settling the group.

Each session has a clearly stated **theme and purpose** that is given at the beginning of the group member's material. After an initial **welcome**, begin by briefly introducing the theme of the session. At the first meeting of the group it is important to give members a chance to introduce themselves (perhaps by talking to the person next to them and introducing them to the whole group). It is also important for the leaders to say a bit more about themselves and the purpose of the course.

Some basic **ground rules** can help such as asking people to come on time for meetings; to send apologies if they can't come; to be courteous if there is disagreement with someone; and to encourage people to ask questions honestly and openly.

Each session begins with **short prayers** in the form of a simple liturgy set out in the member's booklet. One of the group leaders should lead this at the beginning, but you may want to involve the group members as you go through the course. People will arrive with many different things on their minds, and it is important to provide a space for them to settle and to focus in this time set aside on following Jesus Christ. Each member of the group will be at a different place on the journey towards faith. Be sensitive to this. But gently leading people into prayer is one of the best ways of helping them to know God.

Therefore do not skip this part of the session, even if the group is made up of inquirers who are not even sure that they believe in God. A liturgical order for prayer helps here and enables participation much more easily than simply a time of open prayer (though this can form part of the prayer time).

This is also your opportunity to introduce group members to different styles of prayer, and to encourage them to build times of prayer into daily life.

With the welcome the prayers should take about 10 minutes.

There then follows a brief section headed **conversation** in the member's booklet. This is just an icebreaker question to get people thinking and talking. It should only take a few minutes as people buzz and share with each other. It is not intended to be a *long* conversation!

The conversation should last about 5 minutes.

The conversation is followed by a **reflection on Scripture**. There is a Bible passage for each session and over the whole course a breadth and variety of Scripture will be looked at.

The reflective and critical reading of Scripture is a central feature of *Pilgrim*. Our approach to Christian nurture and formation is rooted in Scripture. Together the group learns to read, digest, and reflect on it in ways that will be helpful for the living out of the faith each day as well as understanding what it means. The leader therefore needs to be prepared by having looked at and thought about the passage before the session. The leader is not required to tell the group what the passage means, but to draw out their own responses and questions and then respond to them. There will, of course, be times when explanation is required. Sometimes a guide to this is given in the "essay" that follows. Sometimes the leader will need to provide this. But there are simple explanatory notes on each of the biblical passages in the member's handbook.

By following a similar pattern in each session we hope that when the first stage of the course is completed the group will not necessarily need a leader at all, but will be able to run itself.

This is the pattern for reading Scripture that we ask you to follow in each session. It is based on the ancient monastic way of reading Scripture known as *Lectio Divina* (which simply means godly reading).

- Read the Bible passage through once aloud.

- Invite people to think about it in silence.

- Read the passage again—perhaps asking someone else to read, or divide the passage between different voices. This will depend a bit on the group.

- Invite people to say out loud a word or a phrase from the passage that has struck them. At the beginning make it clear that it's fine to pass and not say anything.

- After a few moments of quiet, read the passage a third time.

- Either in the whole group, or with their neighbor in twos or threes, invite people to share with each other why this word or phrase jumped out at them, what it might mean and what questions it raises.

- Respond as appropriate.

Reflecting on the Scriptures together should take about 30 minutes.

The main teaching content of the session follows. At its heart, each session has a short reflective article. These articles are written by a range of different people: bishops, prominent theologians and church leaders, men and women. Together these reflections form a resource for sharing and reflecting on the Christian faith.

Although the article is not an actual commentary on the Bible passage you have just looked at, it flows from it and helps develop the main theme of the session.

Either read the article aloud or invite people to read it in silence.

In the middle and/or at the end of each article there are questions for discussion. The questions are designed to help the group think creatively about the theme of the session. Make sure you have looked at them in advance and started to think about them before the session begins. Although you are not expected to have all the answers, it is important to have begun thinking about how the session will proceed, and what might come up. By all means add or substitute questions of your own if you think they will work better for your group. Encourage the group to respond in the way that is right for them.

A key part of learning about the Christian faith in this kind of group is the opportunity for group members to ask the questions that are central to their search and journey. After you have looked at the reflection and the questions, we suggest one of the leaders draws this part of the session to a close with a short summary of the theme and then invites questions from the group on this topic or any others they are encountering.

Reading the article and the discussion should take about 30 minutes.

The session concludes with **prayer**. This is a time for a short prayer and also an opportunity for one of the leaders to gather together in prayer the things that have been said and explored in the session.

This emphasis on prayer and reflection in *Pilgrim* is our of recognition that one of the best ways to introduce people to the Christian faith is to provide a place where they feel at ease and can freely ask questions, and where they learn to read the Bible and to pray.

In the final session of each course a slightly longer time of prayer is appropriate. This provides a moment to review the short course, give thanks for what has been learned, and also an opportunity for a response of faith and personal commitment.

The final prayers should be no more than 5 minutes.

The session concludes with a short challenge to live and reflect on what has been explored. Sometimes group members are asked or encouraged to do something practical.

And at the end of each session are a number of quotations from Christian writers and theologians down through the centuries and to the present day. These short readings are included to help demonstrate our participation in a long and unfolding tradition of reading Scripture and pondering the meaning and impact of Jesus Christ, and to enable the group member to go a little deeper into the theme of the session. Encourage people to look at the passages in the coming week.

The final sending out should be no more than 5 minutes.

With refreshments at the beginning and/or the end the whole session should last about an hour and three-quarters; that means a 9:15 pm finish for a session starting at 7:30 pm.

Caring for the people in the group

Some people will come to this course because they want to find out about the Christian faith. They won't necessarily be attending church services at all. Others will come for a kind of refresher course. They will be church goers, but won't necessarily know a lot about their faith. Others will be fringe people, who come to church occasionally.

Becoming a Christian is like a journey. As you lead this group you need to be sensitive to the fact that in each group there will be people at different stages of this journey. Your job is to lead them. In this respect you are their pastor as much as their teacher.

When a group meets for the first time it is important that people are given time to introduce and get to know each other. You also need to be ready to depart from the pattern of the session and be led by the questions and concerns of the group. But you mustn't let any one person's agenda dominate.

Remember that as each session begins, people arrive from busy and often pressured lives and will be carrying some of those concerns with them. This is why refreshments and prayer at the beginning of the session can help. It enables people to wind down and get ready for the session and also share with each other. Our aim is that this little group becomes, in its own distinctive way, a cell or community of the church, enabled, if appropriate, to go on meeting, learning, praying, serving, and supporting each other even after the course has finished.

As you get to know the individuals, try to ensure that each voice is heard and that everyone has the opportunity to speak if they want to. Though bear in mind, being silent doesn't necessarily mean not participating!

Occasionally, someone will talk too much. Have a quiet word with them after a session rather than embarrassing them during it.

Difficult questions will arise. Both tough theological questions and, as the group grows in mutual trust, hard personal matters. If you cannot answer or address the difficult theological questions, be honest about it; make a note of the questions and endeavor to find out for a following session. With personal matters it will sometimes be necessary to see and care for individuals outside the session itself, though the group itself can often be a place where sharing and mutual listening can bring healing solace, and then be offered to God in prayer.

Occasionally people may decide that the group is not for them (which is absolutely fine). Try and make a good ending to their time and leave the door open for people to pick up another group at a future date.

The initial commitment of the group is for six weeks but with a possibility of the group continuing. By at least four weeks in you need to make plans for the next part of the group's life and encourage people to take part. You need to decide as a group of leaders whether to welcome anyone else who wants to join at that point.

You will find that the group has its own life and dynamic as people meet together regularly. The initial group will not know one another. You may want to focus on questions and exercises that help people to tell their story easily. People normally make an effort to be polite but there can be some awkward silences.

As the group gets to know one another better, there will be more to talk about but you may also find people are more honest with one another. Do your best to help the group through conflict and disagreement so they come to appreciate one another.

At that point it can help the life of the group to have a common task such as arranging a meal together or undertaking a simple act of service (such as making the coffee after church on Sunday).

Remember that it does take time for a group of people to form and get to know one another—and normally longer than the initial six-week course.

It may be helpful as the group develops for the leaders to meet occasionally with individual group members outside the group meetings to reflect on how things are going. Not everyone feels able to share or ask questions in a group setting.

Above all, be sensitive to what God is doing in the life of the group and in the life of its members. You will often be surprised and have the sense that you are treading on holy ground here and individuals encounter the love of Christ and the power of the Holy Spirit and their lives are transformed.

"Jesus appointed twelve, whom he named apostles, to be with him and to be sent out..."

MARK 3:14

What is the Grow stage for?

The aim is to help people to learn the essentials for a life of discipleship. A disciple is to be called to live in a rhythm of being with Jesus in community and to be sent out to live out the Christian faith in the whole of his or her life.

Disciples need the support of other Christians and to be part of a community. We need opportunities to reflect and pray together and to explore the riches of our faith. The Grow stage supports that process both for new Christians and for those who have been Christians for many years.

Some groups who use this material will be moving on from the Follow stage of *Pilgrim*. Some will be specially gathered for a short course. Others may be established small groups of different kinds.

How is Grow similar to Follow?

Reading the Bible together slowly, carefully, and prayerfully remains at the heart of this part of *Pilgrim*. The sessions begin and end with prayers. There is a similar structure to the session. There is the same use of quotations from the Christian tradition.

How is Grow different than Follow?

Grow revisits the same four areas as Follow but in greater depth and covering more material. We assume the group are Christians, serious about their discipleship. We have written the materials so that it can be led by members of the group rather than by specially trained leaders. The opening and closing sections of each session are designed to support reflection on the whole life of the disciples.

In the Grow Stage it might be helpful to expand the **opening and closing prayers** with other appropriate material. This can give space to individual gifts and creativity. You may want to allow more time for the opening **conversation** than in the Follow part of *Pilgrim*. Some of the questions invite people to share something of themselves to open up the subject. Others invite people to reflect on their lives over the last week in the light of the theme of the course (except for Session 1 of each course). This is one of the most important habits for a disciple to learn and cannot be rushed. Most groups will be helped by breaking into smaller groups of two or three at this point.

Draw the group back together for the **reading from the Bible** in the normal *Lectio Divina* pattern as in the Follow Stage. Then move from here to the **reflection** on the theme and the **questions** together (again exactly as in the Follow Stage). Most groups will want to work as one group for this part of the session. It will be important to allow more difficult questions to surface. As those leading may not have all the answers, it may be necessary to offer to do some research on hard questions and report back next week.

Journeying on is an additional segment to the sessions in the Grow Stage. Although important, it will not take much time. This is an invitation to carry the theme of this session into the coming week: to watch out for patterns and themes; to put something into practice; to take a question to think about or a pattern for prayer. Journeying sets up the opening conversation for the following session.

The **concluding prayers** can be enriched as appropriate by prayers for the group by singing or an open prayer time as seems right and helpful. **The wisdom for the journey questions** for reflection are for the group to ponder in the coming days.

No small group meeting ever goes according to plan, so keep this structure and your timetable flexible. However, it is the leader's role to keep on bringing the group back to the theme and ensuring that (at least approximately) you stick to the scheduled time.

Are there other ways of using Pilgrim?

We envision that most people will use the Grow material as part of a small group which meets weekly. However, you could also use the material as part of a day retreat or parish weekend.

Review and discernment

It will be important that those leading the group are supported within the wider church and that there are opportunities for the leaders to review and reflect on the life of the group at least a couple of times during the six (or seven) session course.

Helpful questions to ask of each session might be:

● What did we expect to happen?

● What did happen and what were the reasons for this?

● How might we plan differently for the next sessions?

In any group of this kind, the Holy Spirit is at work. You may want to explore what the Spirit is doing in the life of the group and how you can better support people in their own discipleship and journey. You may want to encourage particular gifts that you see emerging. It will also be important to ask, "What next?" (Grow Stage) for this group at the mid-point of the course. Will you go on to another of the *Pilgrim* Grow courses or perhaps use some different material?

Mission and practical tasks

If the group does well, it will begin to form into a community. The bonds of community can be strengthened by undertaking a common task. This might be organizing a community meal. It might be a piece of service to others in the church or neighborhood, perhaps following up the gifts of calling of one or two members of the group, and perhaps links to the theme of the course.

And finally ...

Leading a group for Christians who are exploring discipleship can be demanding but is also immensely rewarding. Make sure the leaders look after one another and pray for one another during the life of the group. Thank you for the service you are offering to your fellow Christians through the life of this small group.

Looking after the practicalities

Welcome. Welcome. Welcome.

The invitation to know Christ is also an invitation to be part of his body, the Church, therefore hospitality, welcome, and sensitivity to the needs of different individuals is central to the whole process of initiation. The truth of our words will be measured by our actions.

So make sure you have a good room to meet in. *Pilgrim* groups will probably meet in people's homes, though it could be in a church hall, a restaurant, or a pub.

Make sure there are refreshments. What is appropriate will vary from group to group, place to place, and session to session. But make sure something is prepared each time. You may decide to have a meal together. There should always be drinks available, either at the beginning or end of the session—or both.

Keep to time. Encourage people to arrive on time. Make sure you finish on time. If some people want to stay on chatting for longer, then this is fine so long as it is okay with the host. But make it clear that others can go if they need to.

pilgrim

PART FOUR:
PILGRIM RESOURCES

Pilgrim Books

The *Pilgrim* program consists of two stages.

Follow Stage

There are four courses in this first Follow Stage of the *Pilgrim* program. The Follow Stage is designed for new inquirers and for those who are very new to faith. Each of these courses consists of six or seven weekly sessions:

- *Turning to Christ*
- *The Lord's Prayer*
- *The Commandments*
- *The Beatitudes*

Grow Stage

The second half the *Pilgrim* program is known as the Grow Stage, because it aims to help readers go further into discipleship and learn more. Like the Follow Stage, the Grow Stage also consists of four courses:

- *The Creed*
- *The Eucharist*
- *The Bible*
- *Church and Kingdom*

This Leader's Guide is designed to assist those leading groups through both stages.

Formats

All titles published as part of the *Pilgrim* program are available in print and in e-book formats. Please visit: www.pilgrimprogram.org.

Liturgical Resources

You will want to pay careful attention to how the group is connected to the wider congregations (or group of congregations) you are part of. This is a two-way process.

It is helpful to make sure that the group is mentioned in the Sunday intercessions as it begins to meet and at key points in its life and not just in the notices.

Once the group has become established you will be able to gain a sense of who may be preparing for baptism or confirmation, or the renewal of baptismal vows. It will be helpful to identify an occasion when this liturgical celebration can happen, including the church and it's location, time and date, and the name of the bishop who will be the celebrant.

For this reason it can be very helpful to celebrate three points in the journey of the group as part of a Sunday service when the community gathers. The Episcopal Church has authorized liturgies for the Admission of Catechumens and Enrollment of Candidates for Baptism. Both of these rites and the explanatory material that accompanies them support the work of catechesis and support disciples in the way of Christ. Both of these can be found in *The Book of Occasional Services* from Church Publishing, 2003.

Concerning the Catechumenate

The catechumenate is a period of training and instruction in Christian understandings about God, human relationships, and the meaning of life, which culminates in the reception of the Sacraments of Christian Initiation.

The systematic instruction and formation of its catechumens is a solemn responsibility of the Christian community. Traditionally, the preparation of catechumens is a responsibility of the bishop, which is shared with the presbyters, deacons, and appointed lay catechists of the diocese.

Principles of implementation

1. A catechumen is defined as an unbaptized adult. These rites are appropriate for use only with such persons.

2. During the period of the catechumenate, the context of catechesis is a continual reflection on Scripture, Christian prayer, worship, and the catechumen's gifts for ministry and work for justice and peace. These elements are more or less a part of each catechetical session.

3. The principal curriculum for each catechetical session is reflection on the respective readings of the Sunday Eucharistic Lectionary as these illumine the faith journey of catechumens, sponsors, and catechists.

4. The catechetical methodology of the catechumenal and baptismal rites is: experience first, then reflect. As the catechumen journeys from inquiry to baptism, there is formation of an ability to discern God's activity in the events of one's life. It is recommended that the services not be discussed prior to their celebration. It is appropriate that sponsors be well prepared for their ministry in the respective services and to guide and support their catechumen during the celebration.

5. The catechumenate exists throughout the year in the parish, and persons may enter at any time. The catechumenate is of undetermined length for each catechumen. The appropriate time for the call to Candidacy for Baptism is discerned by sponsors,

catechists, and clergy on behalf of the local congregation. Baptism of catechumens is normally reserved for the Great Vigil of Easter.

6. Since the catechumenate is ecclesial formation for the ministry of the baptized, it is appropriate that the catechists be representative of the diversity of the local congregation.

7. It is appropriate for those catechumens baptized at the Great Vigil of Easter to join the ministry of sponsor or catechist for new catechumens at the conclusion of the Great Fifty Days.

The Catechumenate is marked by three stages.

Stage 1. The Pre-Catechumenal Period

To this stage belong inquirers' classes with sufficient preparation to enable persons to determine that they wish to become Christians. It is a time during which those who have been initially attracted to the Christian community are guided to examine and test their motives, in order that they may freely commit themselves to pursue a disciplined exploration of the implications of Christian living.

Stage 2. The Catechumenate

Entry into the catechumenate is by a public liturgical act (which may take place for individuals or groups at any time) at the principal Sunday liturgy. Normatively, the act includes signing with the cross. To this stage belong regular association with the worshiping community, the practice of life in accordance with the Gospel (including service to the poor and neglected), encouragement and instruction in the life of prayer, and basic instruction in the history of salvation as revealed in the Holy Scriptures of the Old and New Testaments. This stage will vary in length according to the needs of the individual. For those persons who, although unbaptized, already possess an understanding and appreciation of the Christian religion, it might be relatively short.

Each person to be admitted a catechumen is presented by a sponsor who normally accompanies the catechumen through the process of candidacy and serves as sponsor at Holy Baptism.

Admission to the catechumenate is an appropriate time to determine the name by which one desires to be known in the Christian community. This may be one's given name, a new name legally changed, or an additional name of Christian significance.

From the time of admission, a catechumen is regarded as a part of the Christian community. For example, a person who dies during the catechumenate receives a Christian burial.

Stage 3. Candidacy for Baptism

To this stage belongs a series of liturgical acts leading up to baptism. These ordinarily take place on a series of Sundays preceding one of the stated days for baptism, and involve public prayer for the candidates, who are present at the services as a group, accompanied by their sponsors. When the Sacrament of Holy Baptism is administered at Easter, enrollment as a candidate normally takes place at the beginning of Lent; when baptisms are planned for the Feast of the Baptism of Our Lord, the enrollment takes place at the beginning of Advent.

In addition to these public acts, this stage involves the private disciplines of fasting, examination of conscience, and prayer, in order that the candidates will be spiritually and emotionally ready for baptism. It is appropriate that, in accordance with ancient custom, the sponsors support their candidates by joining them in prayer and fasting.

A fourth period immediately follows the administration of Holy Baptism. In the case of persons baptized at the Great Vigil, it extends over the Fifty Days of Easter. This period is devoted to such activities, formal and informal, as will assist the newly baptized to experience the fullness of the corporate life of the Church and to gain a deeper understanding of the meaning of the Sacraments.

The bishop, the bishop's representative, or the rector (or priest-in-charge) of the congregation should preside at the rites of Admission and Enrollment.

It should be noted that the rites and prayers which follow are appropriate for use only with persons preparing for baptism. Validly baptized Christians present at instruction classes to deepen their understanding of the faith, including members of other Christian bodies preparing to be received into the Episcopal Church, are under no circumstances to be considered catechumens. The same is true of persons preparing to re-affirm their baptismal vows after having abandoned the practice of the Christian religion, since "The bond which God establishes in Baptism is indissoluble" (BCP, 298).

The Presentation of the Four Texts

In order to give shape to their discipleship, all baptized Christians should be encouraged to explore these four texts and make them their own: the Summary of the Law, the Lord's Prayer, the Apostles' Creed, and the Beatitudes. At the heart of *Pilgrim*, they can be presented on cards either within the study group or in public worship, possibly after the sermon, along with a Bible. Below are simple liturgies for the giving of each of these texts to individuals during the course of their study and affirmation of continuing discipleship. According to *The Book of Occasional Services* (pp. 128-9), either the Apostles' or Nicene Creed may be given to candidates immediately following the sermon on the Third Sunday of Lent. In the same manner, the Lord's Prayer can be given on the Fifth Sunday of Lent.

Jesus' Summary of the Law

One of the following or other readings may be used:

Exodus 20:1-19; Leviticus 19:9-18; Romans 8:1-4; Romans 13:8-10; Galatians 5:13,14; Mark 12:28-34

One of the following psalms may be used:

Psalm 1:15; 119:9-16; 119:97-104

The minister addresses those who are disciples on the Way of faith:

Brothers and sisters, listen carefully to the words that Jesus gave us as a summary of the law. These few words help us understand how we are to live as human beings in God's world. They are given not to condemn us but to show how by the grace of God we may live as free people reflecting the goodness and love of God.

The Summary of the Law is read:

Our Lord Jesus Christ said:
"The first commandment is this:
'Hear, O Israel, the Lord our God is the only Lord.
You shall love the Lord your God with all your heart,
with all your soul, with all your mind,
and with all your strength.'
The second is this: 'Love your neighbor as yourself.'
There is no other commandment greater than these.
On these two commandments hang all the law and the prophets."

God of truth,
help us to keep your law of love
and to walk in ways of wisdom,
that we may find true life
in Jesus Christ your Son.

All: Amen.

The Lord's Prayer

One of the following or other readings may be used:

1 Kings 8:27-30; Hosea 11:1-4; Romans 8:14-17, 26, 27; Galatians 4:4-7; Matthew 6:7-13; Luke 11:1-4

One of the following psalms may be used:

Psalm 23; 103:6-18

The minister addresses those who are disciples on the Way of faith:

Brothers and sisters, listen carefully to the Lord's Prayer. It is given to us as a pattern for our praying as well as a prayer that we can make our own. It teaches us that heaven is open to our prayers and that the world is open to the gracious working of God.

The Lord's Prayer is read in the form which is commonly used by the congregation.

Our Father in heaven,
hallowed be your name,
your kingdom come,
your will be done,
on earth as in heaven.
Give us today our daily bread.
Forgive us our sins
as we forgive those who sin against us.
Lead us not into temptation
but deliver us from evil.
For the kingdom, the power,
and the glory are yours
now and for ever.
Amen.

(or)

Our Father, who art in heaven,
hallowed be thy name;
thy kingdom come;

thy will be done;
on earth as it is in heaven.
Give us this day our daily bread.
And forgive us our trespasses,
as we forgive those who trespass against us.
And lead us not into temptation;
but deliver us from evil.
For thine is the kingdom,
the power and the glory,
for ever and ever.
Amen.

The minister says:

Lord of heaven and earth,
as Jesus taught his disciples to be persistent in prayer,
give us patience and courage never to lose hope,
but always to bring our prayers before you;
through Jesus Christ our Lord.

All: Amen.

The Apostles' Creed

One of the following or other readings may be used:

Deuteronomy 6:1-7; Deuteronomy 26:1-10; Romans 10:8-13; 1 Timothy
6:11-16; 2 Timothy 1:8-14; Matthew 16:13-18; John 12:44-50

One of the following psalms may be used:

Psalm 78:1-7; 145:1-9

The minister addresses those who are disciples on the Way of faith:

Brothers and sisters, listen carefully to this declaration of faith, which the Church calls the Apostles' Creed. Christians have said this together since the earliest centuries, especially at baptism, where we confess that Jesus is our Lord and Savior. It speaks of our belief in God's love for the world, in creation, in incarnation, and in salvation.

The Apostles' Creed is read:

I believe in God, the Father almighty,
creator of heaven and earth.
I believe in Jesus Christ, his only Son, our Lord,
who was conceived by the Holy Spirit,
born of the Virgin Mary,
suffered under Pontius Pilate,
was crucified, died, and was buried;
he descended to the dead.
On the third day he rose again;
he ascended into heaven,
he is seated at the right hand of the Father,
and he will come to judge the living and the dead.
I believe in the Holy Spirit,
the holy catholic Church,
the communion of saints,
the forgiveness of sins,
the resurrection of the body,
and the life everlasting.
Amen.

The minister says:

Holy God,
faithful and unchanging:
enlarge our minds with the knowledge of your truth,
and draw us more deeply into the mystery of your love,
that we may truly worship you,
Father, Son and Holy Spirit,
one God, now and for ever.

All: Amen.

The Beatitudes—Blessings of the Gospel

One of the following or other readings may be used:

Isaiah 2:2-4; Isaiah 11:1-10; Ephesians 3:7-13; 2 Corinthians 8:9; 1 John 3:1-3; Revelation 21:22-27; Mark 4:30-32

One of the following psalms may be used:

Psalm 72:1-14; 87; 122

The minister addresses those who are disciples on the Way of faith:

Brothers and sisters, listen carefully to these words from Jesus' Sermon on the Mount. In them he declares the blessings of God's kingdom. He gives us a vision of a world redeemed by love, and the qualities of discipleship, which will bring about that transformation.

The Beatitudes are read from either Matthew or Luke:

Matthew 5:3-10

Blessed are the poor in spirit,
for theirs is the kingdom of heaven.
Blessed are those who mourn,
for they shall be comforted.
Blessed are the meek,
for they shall inherit the earth.
Blessed are those who hunger and thirst after righteousness,
for they shall be satisfied.
Blessed are the merciful,
for they shall obtain mercy.
Blessed are the pure in heart,
for they shall see God.
Blessed are the peacemakers,
for they shall be called children of God.

Blessed are those who suffer persecution for righteousness' sake,
for theirs is the kingdom of heaven.

(or)

Luke 6:20-23

Blessed are you who are poor,
for yours is the kingdom of God.
Blessed are you who are hungry now,
for you will be filled.
Blessed are you who weep now,
for you will laugh.
Blessed are you when people hate you,
and when they exclude you, revile you,
and defame you on account of the Son of Man.
Rejoice in that day and leap for joy,
for surely your reward is great in heaven;
for that is what their ancestors did to the prophets.

The minister says:

Almighty God,
you search us and know us:
may we rely on you in strength
and rest on you in weakness,
now and in all our days;
through Jesus Christ our Lord.

All: Amen.

Preparation of Adults for Holy Baptism:

The Catechumenate

Admission of Catechumens

The admission of catechumens may take place at any time of the year, within a principal Sunday liturgy.

After the sermon (or after the Creed) the Celebrant invites those to be admitted as catechumens to come forward with their sponsors.

The Celebrant then asks the following question of those to be admitted. If desired, the question may be asked of each person individually:

What do you seek?

Answer: Life in Christ.

The Celebrant then says:

Jesus said, "The first commandment is this: Hear, O Israel: The Lord our God is the only Lord. Love the Lord your God with all your heart, with all your soul, and with all your strength. The second is this: Love your neighbor as yourself. There is no other commandment greater than these." Do you accept these commandments?

Answer: I do.

Celebrant: Do you promise to be regular in attending the worship of God and in receiving instruction?

Answer: I do.

Celebrant: Will you open your ears to hear the Word of God and your heart and mind to receive the Lord Jesus?

Answer: I will, with God's help.

The Celebrant then addresses the sponsors:

Will you who sponsor these persons support them by prayer and example and help them to grow in the knowledge and love of God?

Sponsors: I will.

Those to be admitted kneel. The sponsors remain standing, and place a hand upon the shoulder of the one they are sponsoring, while the Celebrant extends a hand toward them and says:

May Almighty God, our heavenly Father, who has put the desire into your hearts to seek the grace of our Lord Jesus Christ, grant you the power of the Holy Spirit to persevere in this intention and to grow in faith and understanding.

People: Amen.

Each of those to be admitted is presented by name to the Celebrant, who, with the thumb, marks a cross on the forehead of each, saying:

N., receive the sign of the Cross on your forehead and in your heart, in the Name of the Father, and of the Son, and of the Holy Spirit.

People: Amen.

The sponsors also mark a cross on the foreheads of their catechumens.

The catechumens and sponsors then return to their places.

The Liturgy continues with (the Creed and) the Prayers of the People, in the course of which prayer is offered for the new catechumens by name.

If any of the catechumens, after consultation with the celebrant, wishes to renounce a former way of worship, an appropriately worded renunciation may be included immediately following the first question and answer.

Enrollment of Candidates for Baptism

The enrollment of candidates for Baptism at the Great Vigil of Easter normally takes place on the First Sunday in Lent. For those preparing for Baptism on the Feast of our Lord's Baptism, it takes place on the First Sunday of Advent.

The large book in which the names of the candidates for Baptism are to be written is placed where it can easily be seen and used.

After the Creed, the catechumens to be enrolled are invited to come forward with their sponsors. A Catechist, or other lay representative of the congregation, presents them to the bishop or priest with the following or similar words:

I present to you these catechumens who have been strengthened by God's grace and supported by the example and prayers of this congregation, and I ask that they be enrolled as candidates for Holy Baptism.

The Celebrant asks the sponsors:

Have they been regular in attending the worship of God and in receiving instruction?

Sponsors: They have. (He has.)

Celebrant: Are they seeking by prayer, study, and example to pattern their lives in accordance with the Gospel?

Sponsors: They are. (He is.)

The Celebrant asks the sponsors and congregation:

As God is your witness, do you approve the enrolling of these catechumens as candidates for Holy Baptism?

Answer: We do.

The Celebrant addresses the catechumens:

Do you desire to be baptized?

Catechumens: I do.

The Celebrant then says:

In the Name of God, and with the consent of this congregation, I accept you as candidates for Holy Baptism, and direct that your names be written in this book. God grant that they may also be written in the Book of Life.

The candidates then publicly write their names in the book; or, if necessary, someone else may write the names. Each name is said aloud at the time of writing. The sponsors may also sign the book.

The candidates remain together at the front of the church while the Deacon, or other person appointed, leads the following litany:

In peace let us pray to the Lord, saying "Lord, have mercy."

For these catechumens, that they may remember this day on which they were chosen, and remain for ever grateful for this heavenly blessing, let us pray to the Lord.

Lord, have mercy.

That they may use this Lenten season wisely, joining with us in acts of self-denial and in performing works of mercy, let us pray to the Lord.

Lord, have mercy.

For their teachers, that they may make known to those whom they teach the riches of the Word of God, let us pray to the Lord.

Lord, have mercy.

For their sponsor(s), that in their private lives and public actions they may show to these candidates a pattern of life in accordance with the Gospel, let us pray to the Lord.

Lord, have mercy.

For their families and friends, that they may place no obstacles in the way of these candidates, but rather assist them to follow the promptings of the Spirit, let us pray to the Lord.

Lord, have mercy.

For this congregation, that [during this Lenten season] it may abound in love and persevere in prayer, let us pray to the Lord.

Lord, have mercy.

For our Bishop, and for all the clergy and people, let us pray to the Lord.

Lord, have mercy.

For our President, for the leaders of the nations, and for all in authority, let us pray to the Lord.

Lord, have mercy.

For the sick and the sorrowful, and for those in any need or trouble, let us pray to the Lord.

Lord, have mercy.

For _____, let us pray to the Lord.

Lord, have mercy.

For all who have died in the hope of the resurrection, and for all the departed, let us pray to the Lord.

Lord, have mercy.

In the communion of [_____ and of all the] saints, let us commend ourselves, and one another, and all our life, to Christ our God.

To you, O Lord our God.

Silence

The Celebrant says the following prayer with hands extended over the candidates:

Immortal God, Lord Jesus Christ, the protector of all who come to you, the life of those who believe, and the resurrection of the dead: We call upon you for these your servants who desire the grace of spiritual rebirth in the Sacrament of Holy Baptism. Accept them, Lord Christ, as you promised when you said, "Ask, and it will be given you; seek, and you will find; knock, and it will be opened to you."

Give now, we pray, to those who ask, let those who seek find, open the gate to those who knock; that these your servants may receive the everlasting benediction of your heavenly washing, and come to that promised kingdom which you have prepared, and where you live and reign for ever and ever. Amen.

Other Books and Resources

Leading Small Groups

Many group leaders will be expert at leading small groups and need no further help, but if you do not feel confident about how to lead a small group effectively you may find the following books helpful.

Arnold, Jeffrey. *The Big Book on Small Groups.* InterVarsity Press Connect, 2004.

Boren, M. Scott. *Leading Small Groups in the Way of Jesus.* InterVarsity Press, 2014

Gladden, Steve. *Small Groups with Purpose: How to Create Healthy Communities.* Baker Books, 2013.

Regan, Jane E. *Forming a Community of Faith: A Guide to Success in Adult Faith Formation Today.* Twenty-Third Publications, 2014.

Seymour, Jack. *Teaching Biblical Faith: Leading Small Group Bible Studies.* Abingdon Press, 2015.

Discovering More about Faith

There may be people in your group who want to read more about the Christian faith. These are good "beginner level" books.

Anderson, Carol. *Knowing Jesus in Your Life.* Morehouse, 1995.

Bell, Rob. *What We Talk About When We Talk About God.* HarperOne, 2013.

Borg, Marcus. *Embracing an Adult Faith: What it Means to be a Christian.* (workbook and DVD) Morehouse Education Resources, 2010.

Curry, Michael B. *Crazy Christians: A Call to Follow Jesus.* Morehouse, 2013.

Gray-Reeves, Mary. *Unearthing My Religion: Real Talk about Real Faith.* Morehouse, 2013.

Lewis, C. S. *Mere Christianity.* Harper San Francisco, 2015.

Webber, Christopher. *Welcome to the Christian Faith.* Morehouse, 2011.

Wright, N. T. *Simply Christian: Why Christianity Makes Sense*. HarperOne, 2010.
Wright, N. T. *Simply Jesus: A New Vision of Who He Was, What He Did, and Why He Matters*. HarperOne, 2011.

These books are more in depth introductions to Christian doctrine:

McGrath, Alister E. *The Christian Theology Reader*, 4th edition. Wiley-Blackwell, 2011.
Migliore, Daniel L. *Faith Seeking Understanding: An Introduction to Christian Theology*, 3rd edition. Wm. B. Eerdmans Publishing, 2014.
Ramsey, Michael *The Anglican Spirit*. Seabury Books, 2004.
Thompsett, Fredrica Harris *We Are Theologians: Strengthening the People of God*. Seabury Books, 2004.

Discovering More about the Bible

One of the main pillars of this course is reading the Bible. Some people may want to learn more about the Bible itself as well as the principles behind *Lectio Divina*.

Black, Vicki K. and Peter Wenner. *Welcome to the Bible*. Morehouse, 2007.
Morgan, Donn. *Talking with the Bible: Scripture As Conversation*. Seabury Books, 2013.
Painter, Christine Valters. *Lectio Divina: The Sacred Art*. Skylight Paths, 2011.
Smith, Martin. *The Word is Very Near You: A Guide to Praying with Scripture*. Cowley, 1989.
Wade, Frank. *Transforming Scripture*. Church Publishing, 2008.

Helpful Handbooks and Introductions for New Christians

Haller, Tobias Stanislas, ed. *The Episcopal Handbook*, revised edition. Morehouse, 2015.
George, Cathy H. *You Are Already Praying: Stories of God at Work*. Morehouse, 2013.

Mayfield, Sue. *Exploring Prayer.* Hendrickson, 2007.

Webber, Christopher L. *Welcome to Sunday: An Introduction to Worship in the Episcopal Church.* Morehouse, 2002.

Westerhoff, John H., III with Sharon Ely Pearson. *A People Called Episcopalians: A Brief Introduction to Our Way of Life*, revised edition. Morehouse, 2014.

Discovering More about The Episcopal Church

This course is very clearly on Episcopal discipleship. For people who want to learn more about The Episcopal Church, the following books will be helpful.

Black, Vicki K. *Welcome to the Book of Common Prayer.* Morehouse, 2005.

Gamber, Jenifer with Bill Lewellis. *Your Faith, Your Life: An Invitation to the Episcopal Church.* Morehouse, 2009.

Law, Eric H. F. and Stephanie Spellers. *The Episcopal Way* (Church's Teachings for a Changing World Series: Volume 1). Morehouse, 2014.

Markham, Ian S. and C. K. Robertson. *Episcopal Questions, Episcopal Answers: Exploring Christian Faith.* Morehouse, 2014.

Webber, Christopher L. *Welcome to the Episcopal Church: An Introduction to Its History, Faith, and Worship.* Morehouse, 1999.

Wells, Samuel. *What Episcopalians Believe: An Introduction.* Morehouse, 2011.

Westerhoff, John H., III. *Living Faithfully as a Prayer Book People.* Morehouse, 2004.

More Detailed Books on Baptism

Kitch, Anne E. *Preparing for Baptism in The Episcopal Church.* Morehouse, 2015.

McLaughlin, Nancy. *Do You Believe? Living the Baptismal Covenant.* Morehouse, 2006.

Tammany, Klara. *Living Water: Baptism as a Way of Life*. Church Publishing, 2002.

Webber, Christopher L. *User's Guide to Baptism and Confirmation*. Morehouse, 2006.

More Detailed Books on the Lord's Prayer

Barclay, William. *The Lord's Prayer.* Westminster Press, 1998.

Crossan, John Dominic. *The Greatest Prayer: Rediscovering the Revolutionary Message of the Lord's Prayer.* HarperOne, 2011.

Donigian, George H. *Three Prayers You'll Want to Pray.* Morehouse, 2014.

Hauerwas, Stanley and William H. Willimon. *Lord, Teach Us: The Lord's Prayer & the Christian Life*. Abingdon, 1996.

Wright, N. T. *The Lord and His Prayer.* Wm. B. Eerdmans, 2014.

More Detailed Books on the Commandments

Chan, Yiu Sing Lucas. *The Ten Commandments and the Beatitudes: Biblical Studies and Ethics for Real Life.* Rowman & Littlefield, 2012.

Hauerwas, Stanley and William H. Willimon *The Truth About God: The Ten Commandments in Christian Life.* Abingdon, 1999.

Robertson, Anne. *God's Top 10: Blowing the Lid Off the Commandments.* Morehouse, 2006.

More Detailed Books on the Beatitudes

Bonhoeffer, Dietrich. *The Cost of Discipleship.* Touchstone, 1995.

Borg, Marcus. *Conversations with Scripture: The Gospel of Mark.* Morehouse, 2009.

Yancey, Philip. *The Jesus I Never Knew.* Zondervan, 2002.

An Outline of the Faith
(commonly called The Catechism)

Human Nature

Q. *What are we by nature?*

A. We are part of God's creation, made in the image of God.

Q. *What does it mean to be created in the image of God?*

A. It means that we are free to make choices: to love, to create, to reason, and to live in harmony with creation and with God.

Q. *Why then do we live apart from God and out of harmony with creation?*

A. From the beginning, human beings have misused their freedom and made wrong choices.

Q. *Why do we not use our freedom as we should?*

A. Because we rebel against God, and we put ourselves in the place of God.

Q. *What help is there for us?*

A. Our help is in God.

Q. *How did God first help us?*

A. God first helped us by revealing himself and his will, through nature and history, through many seers and saints, and especially through the prophets of Israel.

God the Father

Q. *What do we learn about God as creator from the revelation to Israel?*

A. We learn that there is one God, the Father Almighty, creator of heaven and earth, of all that is, seen and unseen.

Q. *What does this mean?*

A. This means that the universe is good, that it is the work of a single loving God who creates, sustains, and directs it.

Q. *What does this mean about our place in the universe?*

A. It means that the world belongs to its creator; and that we are called to enjoy it and to care for it in accordance with God's purposes.

Q. *What does this mean about human life?*

A. It means that all people are worthy of respect and honor, because all are created in the image of God, and all can respond to the love of God.

Q. *How was this revelation handed down to us?*

A. This revelation was handed down to us through a community created by a covenant with God.

The Old Covenant

Q. *What is meant by a covenant with God?*

A. A covenant is a relationship initiated by God, to which a body of people responds in faith.

Q. *What is the Old Covenant?*

A. The Old Covenant is the one given by God to the Hebrew people.

Q.   *What did God promise them?*

A.   God promised that they would be his people to bring all the nations of the world to him.

Q.   *What response did God require from the chosen people?*

A.   God required the chosen people to be faithful; to love justice, to do mercy, and to walk humbly with their God.

Q.   *Where is this Old Covenant to be found?*

A.   The covenant with the Hebrew people is to be found in the books which we call the Old Testament.

Q.   *Where in the Old Testament is God's will for us shown most clearly?*

A.   God's will for us is shown most clearly in the Ten Commandments.

The Ten Commandments

Q.   *What are the Ten Commandments?*

A.   The Ten Commandments are the laws given to Moses and the people of Israel.

Q.   *What do we learn from these commandments?*

A.   We learn two things: our duty to God, and our duty to our neighbors.

Q.   *What is our duty to God?*

A.   Our duty is to believe and trust in God;

I.   To love and obey God and to bring others to know him;

II.   To put nothing in the place of God;

III.   To show God respect in thought, word, and deed;

IV. And to set aside regular times for worship, prayer, and the study of God's ways.

Q. *What is our duty to our neighbors?*

A. Our duty to our neighbors is to love them as ourselves, and to do to other people as we wish them to do to us;

V. To love, honor, and help our parents and family; to honor those in authority, and to meet their just demands;

VI. To show respect for the life God has given us; to work and pray for peace; to bear no malice, prejudice, or hatred in our hearts; and to be kind to all the creatures of God;

VII. To use all our bodily desires as God intended;

VIII. To be honest and fair in our dealings; to seek justice, freedom, and the necessities of life for all people; and to use our talents and possessions as ones who must answer for them to God;

IX. To speak the truth, and not to mislead others by our silence;

X. To resist temptations to envy, greed, and jealousy; to rejoice in other people's gifts and graces; and to do our duty for the love of God, who has called us into fellowship with him.

Q. *What is the purpose of the Ten Commandments?*

A. The Ten Commandments were given to define our relationship with God and our neighbors.

Q. *Since we do not fully obey them, are they useful at all?*

A. Since we do not fully obey them, we see more clearly our sin and our need for redemption.

Sin and Redemption

Q. *What is sin?*

A. Sin is the seeking of our own will instead of the will of God, thus distorting our relationship with God, with other people, and with all creation.

Q. *How does sin have power over us?*

A. Sin has power over us because we lose our liberty when our relationship with God is distorted.

Q. *What is redemption?*

A. Redemption is the act of God which sets us free from the power of evil, sin, and death.

Q. *How did God prepare us for redemption?*

A. God sent the prophets to call us back to himself, to show us our need for redemption, and to announce the coming of the Messiah.

Q. *What is meant by the Messiah?*

A. The Messiah is one sent by God to free us from the power of sin, so that with the help of God we may live in harmony with God, within ourselves, with our neighbors, and with all creation.

Q. *Who do we believe is the Messiah?*

A. The Messiah, or Christ, is Jesus of Nazareth, the only Son of God.

God the Son

Q. *What do we mean when we say that Jesus is the only Son of God?*

A. We mean that Jesus is the only perfect image of the Father, and shows us the nature of God.

Q. *What is the nature of God revealed in Jesus?*

A. God is love.

Q. *What do we mean when we say that Jesus was conceived by the power of the Holy Spirit and became incarnate from the Virgin Mary?*

A. We mean that by God's own act, his divine Son received our human nature from the Virgin Mary, his mother.

Q. *Why did he take our human nature?*

A. The divine Son became human, so that in him human beings might be adopted as children of God, and be made heirs of God's kingdom.

Q. *What is the great importance of Jesus' suffering and death?*

A. By his obedience, even to suffering and death, Jesus made the offering which we could not make; in him we are freed from the power of sin and reconciled to God.

Q. *What is the significance of Jesus' resurrection?*

A. By his resurrection, Jesus overcame death and opened for us the way of eternal life.

Q. *What do we mean when we say that he descended to the dead?*

A. We mean that he went to the departed and offered them also the benefits of redemption.

Q. *What do we mean when we say that he ascended into heaven and is seated at the right hand of the Father?*

A. We mean that Jesus took our human nature into heaven where he now reigns with the Father and intercedes for us.

Q. *How can we share in his victory over sin, suffering, and death?*

A. We share in his victory when we are baptized into the New Covenant and become living members of Christ.

The New Covenant

Q. *What is the New Covenant?*

A. The New Covenant is the new relationship with God given by Jesus Christ, the Messiah, to the apostles; and, through them, to all who believe in him.

Q. *What did the Messiah promise in the New Covenant?*

A. Christ promised to bring us into the kingdom of God and give us life in all its fullness.

Q. *What response did Christ require?*

A. Christ commanded us to believe in him and to keep his commandments.

Q. *What are the commandments taught by Christ?*

A. Christ taught us the Summary of the Law and gave us the New Commandment.

Q. *What is the Summary of the Law?*

A. You shall love the Lord your God with all your heart, with all your soul, and with all your mind. This is the first and the great commandment. And the second is like it: You shall love your neighbor as yourself.

Q. *What is the New Commandment?*

A. The New Commandment is that we love one another as Christ loved us.

Q. *Where may we find what Christians believe about Christ?*

A. What Christians believe about Christ is found in the Scriptures and summed up in the creeds.

The Creeds

Q. *What are the creeds?*

A. The creeds are statements of our basic beliefs about God.

Q. *How many creeds does this Church use in its worship?*

A. This Church uses two creeds: The Apostles' Creed and the Nicene Creed.

Q. *What is the Apostles' Creed?*

A. The Apostles' Creed is the ancient creed of Baptism; it is used in the Church's daily worship to recall our Baptismal Covenant.

Q. *What is the Nicene Creed?*

A. The Nicene Creed is the creed of the universal Church and is used at the Eucharist.

Q. *What, then, is the Athanasian Creed?*

A. The Athanasian Creed is an ancient document proclaiming the nature of the Incarnation and of God as Trinity.

Q. *What is the Trinity?*

A. The Trinity is one God: Father, Son, and Holy Spirit.

The Holy Spirit

Q. *Who is the Holy Spirit?*

A. The Holy Spirit is the Third Person of the Trinity, God at work in the world and in the Church even now.

Q. *How is the Holy Spirit revealed in the Old Covenant?*

A. The Holy Spirit is revealed in the Old Covenant as the giver of life, the One who spoke through the prophets.

Q. *How is the Holy Spirit revealed in the New Covenant?*

A. The Holy Spirit is revealed as the Lord who leads us into all truth and enables us to grow in the likeness of Christ.

Q. *How do we recognize the presence of the Holy Spirit in our lives?*

A. We recognize the presence of the Holy Spirit when we confess Jesus Christ as Lord and are brought into love and harmony with God, with ourselves, with our neighbors, and with all creation.

Q. *How do we recognize the truths taught by the Holy Spirit?*

A. We recognize truths to be taught by the Holy Spirit when they are in accord with the Scriptures.

The Holy Scriptures

Q. *What are the Holy Scriptures?*

A. The Holy Scriptures, commonly called the Bible, are the books of the Old and New Testaments; other books, called the Apocrypha, are often included in the Bible.

Q. *What is the Old Testament?*

A. The Old Testament consists of books written by the people of the Old Covenant, under the inspiration of the Holy Spirit, to show God at work in nature and history.

Q. *What is the New Testament?*

A. The New Testament consists of books written by the people of the New Covenant, under the inspiration of the Holy Spirit, to set forth the life and teachings of Jesus and to proclaim the Good News of the Kingdom for all people.

Q. *What is the Apocrypha?*

A. The Apocrypha is a collection of additional books written by people of the Old Covenant, and used in the Christian Church.

Q. *Why do we call the Holy Scriptures the Word of God?*

A. We call them the Word of God because God inspired their human authors and because God still speaks to us through the Bible.

Q. *How do we understand the meaning of the Bible?*

A. We understand the meaning of the Bible by the help of the Holy Spirit, who guides the Church in the true interpretation of the Scriptures.

The Church

Q. *What is the Church?*

A. The Church is the community of the New Covenant.

Q. *How is the Church described in the Bible?*

A. The Church is described as the Body of which Jesus Christ is the Head and of which all baptized persons are members. It is called the People of God, the New Israel, a holy nation, a royal priesthood, and the pillar and ground of truth.

Q. *How is the Church described in the creeds?*

A. The Church is described as one, holy, catholic, and apostolic.

Q. *Why is the Church described as one?*

A. The Church is one, because it is one Body, under one Head, our Lord Jesus Christ.

Q. *Why is the Church described as holy?*

A. The Church is holy, because the Holy Spirit dwells in it, consecrates its members, and guides them to do God's work.

Q. *Why is the Church described as catholic?*

A. The Church is catholic, because it proclaims the whole Faith to all people, to the end of time.

Q. *Why is the Church described as apostolic?*

A. The Church is apostolic, because it continues in the teaching and fellowship of the apostles and is sent to carry out Christ's mission to all people.

Q. *What is the mission of the Church?*

A. The mission of the Church is to restore all people to unity with God and each other in Christ.

Q. *How does the Church pursue its mission?*

A. The Church pursues its mission as it prays and worships, proclaims the Gospel, and promotes justice, peace, and love.

Q. *Through whom does the Church carry out its mission?*

A. The Church carries out its mission through the ministry of all its members.

The Ministry

Q. *Who are the ministers of the Church?*

A. The ministers of the Church are lay persons, bishops, priests, and deacons.

Q. *What is the ministry of the laity?*

A. The ministry of lay persons is to represent Christ and his Church; to bear witness to him wherever they may be; and, according to the gifts given them, to carry on Christ's work of reconciliation in the world; and to take their place in the life, worship, and governance of the Church.

Q. *What is the ministry of a bishop?*

A. The ministry of a bishop is to represent Christ and his Church, particularly as apostle, chief priest, and pastor of a diocese; to guard the faith, unity, and discipline of the whole Church; to proclaim the Word of God; to act in Christ's name for the reconciliation of the world and the building up of the Church; and to ordain others to continue Christ's ministry.

Q. *What is the ministry of a priest or presbyter?*

A. The ministry of a priest is to represent Christ and his Church, particularly as pastor to the people; to share with the bishop in the overseeing of the Church; to proclaim the Gospel; to administer the sacraments; and to bless and declare pardon in the name of God.

Q. *What is the ministry of a deacon?*

A. The ministry of a deacon is to represent Christ and his Church, particularly as a servant of those in need; and to assist bishops and priests in the proclamation of the Gospel and the administration of the sacraments.

Q. *What is the duty of all Christians?*

A. The duty of all Christians is to follow Christ; to come together week by week for corporate worship; and to work, pray, and give for the spread of the kingdom of God.

Prayer and Worship

Q. *What is prayer?*

A. Prayer is responding to God, by thought and by deeds, with or without words.

Q. *What is Christian Prayer?*

A. Christian prayer is response to God the Father, through Jesus Christ, in the power of the Holy Spirit.

Q. *What prayer did Christ teach us?*

A. Our Lord gave us the example of prayer known as the Lord's Prayer.

Q. *What are the principal kinds of prayer?*

A. The principal kinds of prayer are adoration, praise, thanksgiving, penitence, oblation, intercession, and petition.

Q. *What is adoration?*

A. Adoration is the lifting up of the heart and mind to God, asking nothing but to enjoy God's presence.

Q. *Why do we praise God?*

A. We praise God, not to obtain anything, but because God's Being draws praise from us.

Q. *For what do we offer thanksgiving?*

A. Thanksgiving is offered to God for all the blessings of this life, for our redemption, and for whatever draws us closer to God.

Q. *What is penitence?*

A. In penitence, we confess our sins and make restitution where possible, with the intention to amend our lives.

Q. *What is prayer of oblation?*

A. Oblation is an offering of ourselves, our lives and labors, in union with Christ, for the purposes of God.

Q. *What are intercession and petition?*

A. Intercession brings before God the needs of others; in petition, we present our own needs, that God's will may be done.

Q. *What is corporate worship?*

A. In corporate worship, we unite ourselves with others to acknowledge the holiness of God, to hear God's Word, to offer prayer, and to celebrate the sacraments.

The Sacraments

Q. *What are the sacraments?*

A. The sacraments are outward and visible signs of inward and spiritual grace, given by Christ as sure and certain means by which we receive that grace.

Q. *What is grace?*

A. Grace is God's favor towards us, unearned and undeserved; by grace God forgives our sins, enlightens our minds, stirs our hearts, and strengthens our wills.

Q. *What are the two great sacraments of the Gospel?*

A. The two great sacraments given by Christ to his Church are Holy Baptism and the Holy Eucharist.

Holy Baptism

Q. *What is Holy Baptism?*

A. Holy Baptism is the sacrament by which God adopts us as his children and makes us members of Christ's Body, the Church, and inheritors of the kingdom of God.

Q. *What is the outward and visible sign in Baptism?*

A. The outward and visible sign in Baptism is water, in which the person is baptized in the Name of the Father, and of the Son, and of the Holy Spirit.

Q. *What is the inward and spiritual grace in Baptism?*

A. The inward and spiritual grace in Baptism is union with Christ in his death and resurrection, birth into God's family the Church, forgiveness of sins, and new life in the Holy Spirit.

Q. *What is required of us at Baptism?*

A. It is required that we renounce Satan, repent of our sins, and accept Jesus as our Lord and Savior.

Q. *Why then are infants baptized?*

A. Infants are baptized so that they can share citizenship in the Covenant, membership in Christ, and redemption by God.

Q. *How are the promises for infants made and carried out?*

A. Promises are made for them by their parents and sponsors, who guarantee that the infants will be brought up within the Church, to know Christ and be able to follow him.

The Holy Eucharist

Q. *What is the Holy Eucharist?*

A. The Holy Eucharist is the sacrament commanded by Christ for the continual remembrance of his life, death, and resurrection, until his coming again.

Q. *Why is the Eucharist called a sacrifice?*

A. Because the Eucharist, the Church's sacrifice of praise and thanksgiving, is the way by which the sacrifice of Christ is made present, and in which he unites us to his one offering of himself.

Q. *By what other names is this service known?*

A. The Holy Eucharist is called the Lord's Supper, and Holy Communion; it is also known as the Divine Liturgy, the Mass, and the Great Offering.

Q. *What is the outward and visible sign in the Eucharist?*

A. The outward and visible sign in the Eucharist is bread and wine, given and received according to Christ's command.

Q. *What is the inward and spiritual grace given in the Eucharist?*

A. The inward and spiritual grace in the Holy Communion is the Body and Blood of Christ given to his people, and received by faith.

Q. *What are the benefits which we receive in the Lord's Supper?*

A. The benefits we receive are the forgiveness of our sins, the strengthening of our union with Christ and one another, and the foretaste of the heavenly banquet which is our nourishment in eternal life.

Q. *What is required of us when we come to the Eucharist?*

A. It is required that we should examine our lives, repent of our sins, and be in love and charity with all people.

Other Sacramental Rites

Q. *What other sacramental rites evolved in the Church under the guidance of the Holy Spirit?*

A. Other sacramental rites which evolved in the Church include confirmation, ordination, holy matrimony, reconciliation of a penitent, and unction.

Q. *How do they differ from the two sacraments of the Gospel?*

A. Although they are means of grace, they are not necessary for all persons in the same way that Baptism and the Eucharist are.

Q. *What is Confirmation?*

A. Confirmation is the rite in which we express a mature commitment to Christ, and receive strength from the Holy Spirit through prayer and the laying on of hands by a bishop.

Q. *What is required of those to be confirmed?*

A. It is required of those to be confirmed that they have been baptized, are sufficiently instructed in the Christian Faith, are penitent for their sins, and are ready to affirm their confession of Jesus Christ as Savior and Lord.

Q. *What is Ordination?*

A. Ordination is the rite in which God gives authority and the grace of the Holy Spirit to those being made bishops, priests, and deacons, through prayer and the laying on of hands by bishops.

Q. *What is Holy Matrimony?*

A. Holy Matrimony is Christian marriage, in which the woman and man enter into a life-long union, make their vows before God and the Church, and receive the grace and blessing of God to help them fulfill their vows.

Q. *What is Reconciliation of a Penitent?*

A. Reconciliation of a Penitent, or Penance, is the rite in which those who repent of their sins may confess them to God in the presence of a priest, and receive the assurance of pardon and the grace of absolution.

Q. *What is Unction of the Sick?*

A. Unction is the rite of anointing the sick with oil, or the laying on of hands, by which God's grace is given for the healing of spirit, mind, and body.

Q. *Is God's activity limited to these rites?*

A. God does not limit himself to these rites; they are patterns of countless ways by which God uses material things to reach out to us.

Q. *How are the sacraments related to our Christian hope?*

A. Sacraments sustain our present hope and anticipate its future fulfillment.

The Christian Hope

Q. *What is the Christian hope?*

A. The Christian hope is to live with confidence in newness and fullness of life, and to await the coming of Christ in glory, and the completion of God's purpose for the world.

Q. *What do we mean by the coming of Christ in glory?*

A. By the coming of Christ in glory, we mean that Christ will come, not in weakness but in power, and will make all things new.

Q. *What do we mean by heaven and hell?*

A. By heaven, we mean eternal life in our enjoyment of God; by hell, we mean eternal death in our rejection of God.

Q. *Why do we pray for the dead?*

A. We pray for them, because we still hold them in our love, and because we trust that in God's presence those who have chosen to serve him will grow in his love, until they see him as he is.

Q. *What do we mean by the last judgment?*

A. We believe that Christ will come in glory and judge the living and the dead.

Q. *What do we mean by the resurrection of the body?*

A. We mean that God will raise us from death in the fullness of our being, that we may live with Christ in the communion of the saints.

Q. *What is the communion of saints?*

A. The communion of saints is the whole family of God, the living and the dead, those whom we love and those whom we hurt, bound together in Christ by sacrament, prayer, and praise.

Q. *What do we mean by everlasting life?*

A. By everlasting life, we mean a new existence, in which we are united with all the people of God, in the joy of fully knowing and loving God and each other.

Q. *What, then, is our assurance as Christians?*

A. Our assurance as Christians is that nothing, not even death, shall separate us from the love of God which is in Christ Jesus our Lord. Amen.

The Baptismal Covenant

Celebrant: Do you believe in God the Father?
People: I believe in God, the Father almighty,
    creator of heaven and earth.

Celebrant: Do you believe in Jesus Christ, the Son of God?
People: I believe in Jesus Christ, his only Son, our Lord.
    He was conceived by the power of the Holy Spirit
        and born of the Virgin Mary.
    He suffered under Pontius Pilate,
        was crucified, died, and was buried.
    He descended to the dead.
    On the third day he rose again.
    He ascended into heaven,
        and is seated at the right hand of the Father.
    He will come again to judge the living and the dead.

Celebrant: Do you believe in God the Holy Spirit?
People: I believe in the Holy Spirit,
    the holy catholic Church,
    the communion of saints,
    the forgiveness of sins,
    the resurrection of the body,
    and the life everlasting.

Celebrant: Will you continue in the apostles' teaching and
fellowship, in the breaking of bread, and in the
prayers?
People: I will, with God's help.

Celebrant: Will you persevere in resisting evil, and, whenever
you fall into sin, repent and return to the Lord?
People: I will, with God's help.

Celebrant: Will you proclaim by word and example the Good news of
God in Christ?
People: I will, with God's help.

Celebrant: Will you seek and serve Christ in all persons, loving your neighbor as yourself?

People: I will, with God's help.

Celebrant: Will you strive for justice and peace among all people, and respect the dignity of every human being?

People: I will, with God's help.

The Five Marks of Mission

The Five Marks of Mission, developed by the Anglican Consultative Council between 1984 and 1990, have won wide acceptance among Anglicans, including those in The Episcopal Church, and have given congregations and dioceses around the world a practical and memorable "checklist" for mission activities.

The Mission of the Church Is the Mission of Christ

- To proclaim the Good News of the Kingdom

- To teach, baptize and nurture new believers

- To respond to human need by loving service

- To seek to transform unjust structures of society, to challenge violence of every kind and to pursue peace and reconciliation

- To strive to safeguard the integrity of creation and sustain and renew the life of the earth

pilgrim

PART FIVE

AND FINALLY...

Three Images of the Catechist

Paul writes extensively about the work of growing new Christians in 1 Corinthians 3. In this chapter the apostles use three interlocking images to present the role of the catechist in the growth and life of those who are coming to faith. Each image is deeply rooted in the biblical tradition of teaching and learning the faith.

> The first is the image of the parent: And so brothers and sisters, I could not speak to you as spiritual people but rather as people of the flesh, as infants in Christ. I fed you with milk, not solid food.
>
> 1 CORINTHIANS 3:1

This image of the parent emphasizes the deep bonds of love between those who are called to teach the faith and those who are learning the faith. It communicates the need for gentleness and nurture and for particular care to be given to nourish those who are new to faith.

The second image is that of gardeners or farmers working together to see the harvest:

> I planted, Apollos watered, but God gave the growth. So neither the one who plants nor the one who waters is anything but only God who gives the growth. The one who plants and the one who waters have a common purpose and each will receive wages according to the labors of each. For we are God's servants working together; you are God's field, God's building.
>
> 1 CORINTHIANS 3:6-9

This image emphasizes the regular, seasonal nature of catechesis in the life of the Church. We should be sowing the seed of the gospel, planting and watering and seeing a harvest of people brought into the kingdom of God on a regular basis (Matthew 9:37). The image emphasizes collaboration: this is not the work of a single minister but of ministers working together each with different tasks. The image emphasizes also the dedication and hard work required in the task before us.

The third image is one of building:

> According to the grace of God given to me, like a skilled master builder I laid a foundation and someone else is building on it. Each builder must choose with care how to build on it. For no one can lay any foundation other than the one that has been laid; that foundation is Jesus Christ.
>
> 1 CORINTHIANS 3:10-11

Again the image speaks of steady, skilled work and of different roles within the overall task of making disciples. It speaks of the prime importance of centering our catechesis on the foundation of Jesus Christ. Yet there is another important element introduced into this image. The builder to whom Paul hands on this work as the architect or master builder is not another minister but the disciple. Although we need the help of others to begin the Way and the support of the Body of Christ to continue in the Way, each one of us is the builder with prime responsibility for our own discipleship. We are building, with the support of the whole Church, God's temple.

This means that catechesis has as its end goal not only mature disciples but disciples who are able to take responsibility for their own Christian lives and vocation and to live out their discipleship in the world.

> O gracious and holy Father;
> give us wisdom to perceive you,
> diligence to seek you,
> patience to wait for you,
> eyes to behold you
> a heart to meditate upon you
> and a life to proclaim you,
> through the power of the Spirit
> of Jesus Christ our Lord
>
> BENEDICT OF NURSIA (C. 550)

NOTES

Page 10: "An Outline of the Faith" from *The Book of Common Prayer* (Church Publishing, 1979), 845-862.

Page 10: *Catechism of the Catholic Church* (Burns and Oates, 2000).

Page 50: Concerning the Catechumenate from *The Book of Occasional Services* (Church Publishing, 2003), 114-116.

Page 50: Admission of Catechumens from *The Book of Occasional Services* (Church Publishing, 2003), 116-118.

Page 50: Enrollment of Candidates for Baptism from *The Book of Occasional Services* (Church Publishing, 2003), 122-125.

Page 54: The Presentation of the Four Texts found in *Common Worship: Christian Initiation* (The Archbishops' Council, Church House Publishing, 2006)

Page 91: The Baptismal Covenant from *The Book of Common Prayer* (Church Publishing, 1979), 304-5 The third image is one of building: